Hillier

Selected Works

ORO Editions
Publishers of Architecture, Art, and Design
Gordon Goff: Publisher

www.oroeditions.com
info@oroeditions.com

Published by ORO Editions

Graphic Design: Pablo Mandel / CircularStudio
ORO Managing Editor: Kirby Anderson

10 9 8 7 6 5 4 3 2 1 First Edition

Library of Congress data available upon request. World Rights: Available

ISBN: 978-1-957183-50-3

Color Separations and Printing: ORO Editions, Inc.
Printed in China.

International Distribution: www.oroeditions.com/distribution

ORO Editions makes a continuous effort to minimize the overall carbon footprint of its publications. As part of this goal, ORO Editions, in association with Global ReLeaf, arranges to plant trees to replace those used in the manufacturing of the paper produced for its books. Global ReLeaf is an international campaign run by American Forests, one of the world's oldest nonprofit conservation organizations. Global ReLeaf is American Forests' education and action program that helps individuals, organizations, agencies, and corporations improve the local and global environment by planting and caring for trees.

Hillier

Selected Works

FOREWORD BY STAN ALLEN

ORO

THIS MONOGRAPH IS DEDICATED
TO THE MEMORY OF BARBARA ANN HILLIER, AIA
JUNE 20, 1951 – NOVEMBER 21, 2022

Table of Contents

Foreword

BY STAN ALLEN

HILLIER: ARCHITECTURE AS VOCATION

Delicately poised between the art of design and the science of building, architecture is a paradoxical field of endeavor. The architect's knowledge is, of necessity, broad rather than deep. An architect proposes creative solutions to complex problems, leading some to the mistaken notion that the architect is a kind of artist. Architects work with technology, from the elemental stacking of bricks to sophisticated computational methods, leading others to the (equally mistaken) idea that architecture is a technical discipline. It is, in fact, the ability to work simultaneously in the artistic and the technical realms that distinguishes the work of the architect. Architecture is a synthetic discipline above all.

Architecture is a visual medium, but architects work with words too, both spoken and written. Buildings and cities shape the landscape of civic life and the architect needs to communicate with an engaged public: not only clients, but local communities, stakeholders, and regulatory agencies. Architecture, unlike painting or sculpture, is fixed in place and persists over time; an architect needs a keen sense of place—that indefinable intuition of *genius loci*. And an architect needs a head for business, otherwise it's all fantasy, private, and never realized.

To be an architect, then, is more than a career choice. More, even, than a passion, as passions can be fleeting, and architecture is a slow and demanding discipline. To be an architect is something closer, I would argue, to a vocation: a kind of calling, that extends beyond the long working hours to encompass an entire outlook on the world. Dictionary definitions of vocation emphasize this idea of a summons to a particular course of action. The Latin word-root is the verb *vocare*, to call, and it is a word often used in the context of a divine call to the religious life. As such, a vocation implies both that the work is worthwhile, and that it requires great dedication—as is the case with the practice of architecture.

The idea of suitability is often evoked—that is to say, that the abilities of the person are perfectly fitted to their chosen vocation. I can think of no better description of Bob and Barbara Hillier, and by extension the work of Hillier, than to refer to this idea of *architecture as vocation*. A vocation, as personal as it is, also implies a wider purpose; architecture is, above all, a social enterprise. To design a building or to plan a fragment of a city is to intervene in the world in hopes of leaving it a better place. Something akin to the Hippocratic oath of "First, do no harm."

Buildings are realized through a complex collaborative process involving clients, designers, consultants, builders, and a community of users. Any partnership rests on dialogue, and at Hillier, that dialogue extends to collaborators and clients. Finally, architecture has a unique ability among the plastic arts to actually improve lives: to give back to society. If we look at the building types that have been at the core of Hillier's practice for more than fifty years we find libraries, laboratories and schools; places for work, healthcare, public institutions, and places to live. The social change that architecture implements is incremental, not revolutionary. Each of these building types has the capacity to concretely improve people's lives, in modest yet significant ways.

These two core ideas—architecture's capacity to better the lives of those who come in contact with it, and the concept of architecture as a vocation—are exemplified by the firm's longstanding commitment to education. I am thinking here not only of Bob's activities as a speaker and an influential teacher at Princeton, but a history of innovative designs for educational facilities dating back to 1974, and the completion of the American International School in Vienna—the first of 12 international secondary schools designed by Hillier. Schools and educational facilities have been at the center of the practice ever since, most recently with the Kirby Math and Science Center at The Lawrenceville School, a building that extended an earlier Hillier design. For an architect to imagine and to construct places where young people are taught—where ideas are discovered and minds are formed—is to give back to society in a meaningful way. Schools are the places where thoughtful and informed citizens are cultivated, our best hope for the preservation of democracy.

Among the firm's many buildings for secondary schools, the Abbe Science Center at the Solebury School in Bucks County, Pennsylvania, is, at first glance, an unassuming structure. This pitched-roof, wood-clad structure pays homage to its rural context. It recalls a barn or a corn-crib. But that first impression is deceptive. This is an intricate building that accommodates a complex program of classrooms, common areas and laboratories. It responds to its built context as much as to the natural landscape. The building's "L" shape creates defined exterior spaces and multiple points of entry. The building offers distinctive prospects to the viewer, enlivening the experience of moving around and through it. These surfaces are in turn articulated with variations of wood cladding, the detailing of each one recalling, while never mimicking, the traditional clapboard of the local vernacular. At the entry nearest the campus the structure opens up to create a shaded porch, and the siding becomes open slats, creating subtle transparencies and shadow patterns. The building adjusts to the gentle slope of the site, taking advantage of the level change to create a double-height entry space—a thoroughly modern and unexpected intervention in the deceptively modest vernacular idiom.

Laboratory buildings are also a place of learning and discovery, and they have played an important role in Hillier's practice. Bob Hillier is well-positioned to understand the culture of the research laboratory: his father James Hillier was a scientist who worked for many years at the RCA research laboratories in Princeton, and (among many other accomplishments), is credited for his role in developing the scanning electron microscope.

The Cornell Ornithology Center is a more elaborate building than the Abbe Science Center, but this reflects the complexity of the program and the site, rather than any desire for formal expression. The footprint of the building was largely dictated by wetland mapping and the need to integrate the building into its natural landscape. The site plan includes pathways, extensive planting, gardens, and terraces. It too offers multiple prospects, but in this case, it is as much the view from inside to out, as the exterior appearance of the building. Ornithology is less a laboratory-based experimental field than it is a science of observation and data gathering: the Cornell lab houses the world's largest library of recorded bird calls, for example. Hillier have designed a building that highlights the many and varied prospects of the natural landscape surrounding the lab. It is a project that highlights the firm's sensitivity both to place and to the intricacies of functional programing.

Any practice is shaped by its time and place, and Hillier is no exception. However, what is remarkable in this case is the consistency of the work that has been developed over more than fifty years. During the 1970s and '80s, when modernist ideas of function and materials were questioned, Hillier's commitment to these modernist ideals never wavered. Architecture could never be an empty rhetorical practice for Hillier, and the firm was never seduced by post-modern eclecticism.

I think there are several reasons for this. The first is the influence of Jean Labatut, Bob's teacher at Princeton, and later his first employer. Labatut, described by Le Corbusier on the occasion of his 1935 visit to Princeton as "an intelligent and liberal-spirited Frenchman,"[1] was a Beaux-Arts trained architect who taught at Princeton from the late 1920's through the 1960s. He has been described as the person most responsible for the high standing of Princeton's School of Architecture at that time. Long before post-modernism, Labatut encouraged a synthesis of modernist ideals with a respect for history and place; it is no coincidence that Robert Venturi also studied at Princeton with Labatut. Bob Hillier, in other words, was perhaps not seduced by post-modernism in those years because he understood precisely where it was coming from, and had a more robust idea of history and place to fall back on.

The other, perhaps less obvious but equally important reason is the significance of the firm's base in the town of Princeton. At times Hillier has had branch offices in Philadelphia, New York, Tampa, and even Shanghai, but Princeton has always been the base. Beyond the University, Princeton hosts many scientific and research laboratories, primarily in the fields of pharmaceuticals and electronics (which of course is what brought the Hillier family to Princeton in the first place). Working slightly outside the metropolitan mainstream, in a milieux dedicated to education and scientific research has, I believe, had a lasting impact on the culture of the firm.

It would be impossible in a short introduction such as this to do justice to the full catalog of Hillier's production; one example will have to stand in for the range and diversity of the firm's production. The co-generation plant at JFK is a building I long admired without knowing who the architect was. And this is fitting. In an era of so-called star architects, the co-generation plant is a building that caught my eye and enlivened an otherwise unpleasant trip to the airport, even though, at the time, its architect was unknown to me. It calls attention to the working infrastructure of the airport more than to a stylistic signature.

To give an anonymous piece of infrastructure a distinctive and elegant presence—a presence that necessarily needs to be understood at distance and at the speed of a passing car—is a statement of faith in architecture's capacity to render the modern civic landscape intelligible. The materials and detailing of the co-generation plant foreground the functional nature of the structure, yet the form recalls that of nearby terminals: machines and people are each housed with equal dignity, and the banal landscape of the airport is enhanced for the weary traveler. The JFK co-generation plant is one of several that the firm has designed and these structures quietly, and without pretense, call attention to Hillier's longstanding commitment to energy use and sustainability.

Looking back on these fifty-plus years dedicated to education, research and scientific discovery, it is only fitting that in 2019 the New Jersey Institute of Technology renamed its architecture and design school the J. Robert and Barbara A. Hillier College of Architecture and Design. With this honor, the firm's commitment to education—both the education of the next generation of architects but also education as a larger commitment to the betterment of society—has been recognized and reaffirmed.

1 Le Corbusier, *When the Cathedrals Were White,*
(New York, McGraw Hill, 1964; French original 1938), p. 140.

Introduction

BY J. ROBERT HILLIER

Welcome!

It is a pleasure to welcome you to the second monograph published by Hillier in our 57 years of practice. You will find within these pages, the projects that we have completed within the last 25 years and also a more retrospective historic section of work going back to our beginnings in the 1960s. We have also included a year-by-year timeline of the growth of the firm marked by major projects and changes in the firm's logo which you will find interesting and perhaps amusing.

I believe that architecture is one of the most exciting professions in which to spend a lifetime and I am so grateful that I found it as a career. It is a profession that is project oriented, and each project is different in that it has a different client, a different program, and a different site in a different context. Each of these elements has to be explored, defined, and listened to—yes, even the site has a story to tell.

My belief is that the best designs come out of a thorough programming process that defines the problem at hand. Just as one programs a computer to do a certain job, one needs to program a building to do its job.

An important part of the program is understanding the "forces" at work on the project. I often refer to them as the "hidden clients." These are forces beyond the usual gravity, weather, and sustainability which confront every building, but are more subtle. They can include culture, history, context, economics, market, codes, and, in some cases, even politics.

As a firm, we believe the architect, working with the client, needs to understand the scope, strength, and priority of each of these forces. We also believe it is the responsibility of the architect to bring all of those forces into balance for a successful final project. As a result you are serving the client, serving society, and serving nature.

This philosophy of design results in every building being unto itself. We cannot have a singular design language because we do not work with a single type of client nor within a single geographical context. In our firm we try to create an environment where each designer and their team can find their own way, unencumbered by some super language or doctrine with which they have to abide. The only doctrine we prescribe is quality and excellence.

Many talented designers, architects, engineers, contractors, and craftspeople contributed to the works in this book. Viewing them retrospectively, I am astonished by the quantity and the quality of the work we have completed over the years, of which this is only a small sample. The title of the book, Selected Works, is intended both, as a reminder of the immense effort that goes into realizing a successful project, and as a tribute to those responsible.

I do want to acknowledge and thank the team that created this book. They are Julian Edgren, Caryn Farnum, Julia Stanat, Kaitlyn Zook, and their leader in this effort, Alexander Kim.

I hope that you enjoy these pages and the work therein.

Opposite: *Autretemps* rendered plan by Sanda Iliescu

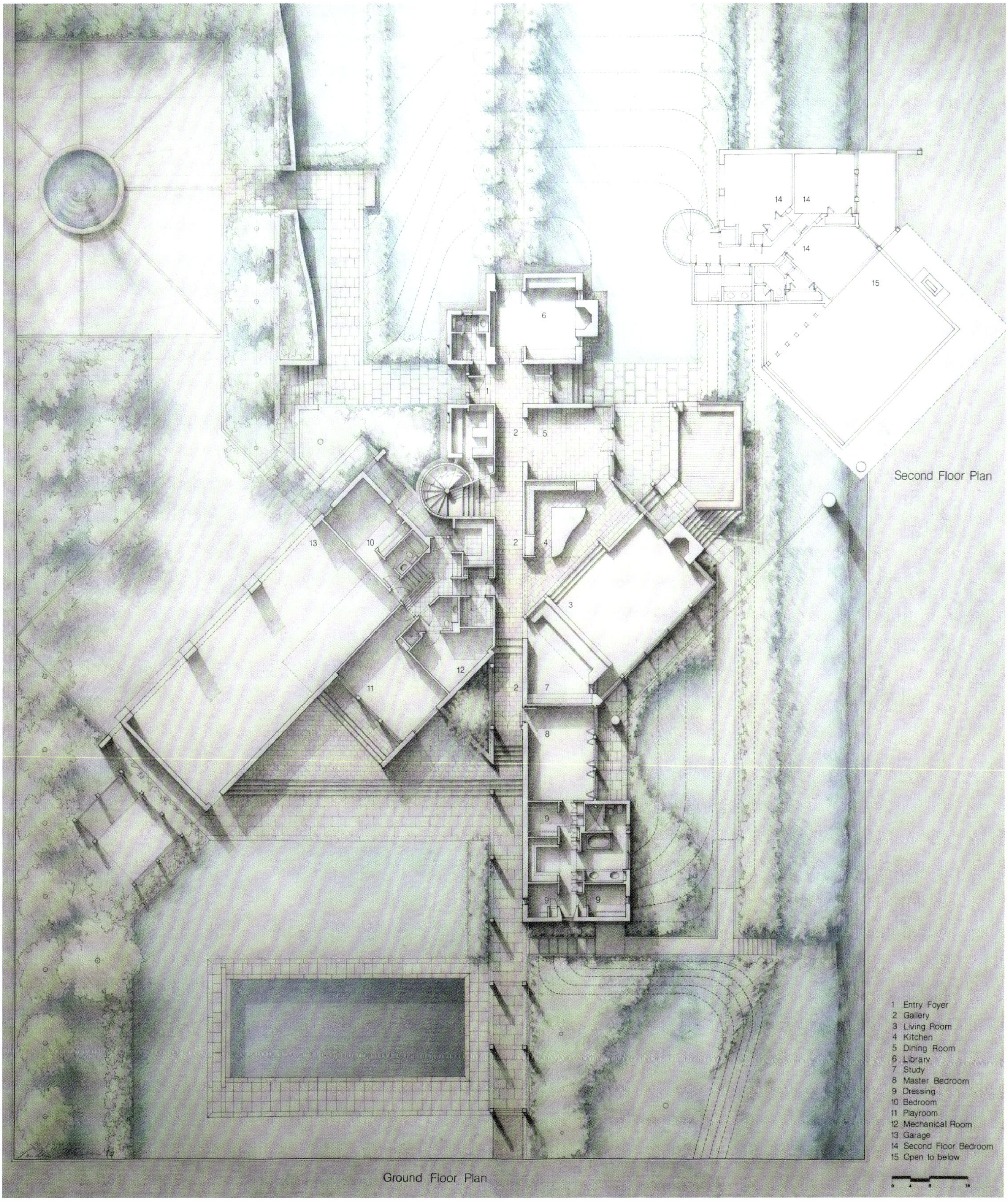

Second Floor Plan
Ground Floor Plan
1 Entry Foyer
2 Gallery
3 Living Room
4 Kitchen
5 Dining Room
6 Library
7 Study
8 Master Bedroom
9 Dressing
10 Bedroom
11 Playroom
12 Mechanical Room
13 Garage
14 Second Floor Bedroom
15 Open to below

Projects

Autretemps

NEW HOPE, PA
6,000 SF

Autretemps is a spectacular stone and glass house sited on twenty-two wooded acres between the Delaware Canal and the Delaware River. From the front it presents itself as "stone boxes"—solid masses with thick walls and few punctures. On the river side, the massive stone walls peel away, allowing the structural skeleton to break loose. Columns, trusses, and beams stretch out past the boundaries of the spatial volumes to meet the Delaware.

Inside, the organization takes advantage of the spectacular river views. Living, dining, and sleeping areas, which are arranged in a linear sequence, can be accessed from a prominent circulation spine and gallery that parallels the river. The stairway to the second level is wrapped in a glass silo that is lit at night. The living room, kitchen, and study comprise a single articulated space that is the operating core of the house.

LVMH Tower

NEW YORK, NY
106,000 SF

Hillier collaborated with Christian de Portzamparc, a Pritzker Prize-winning architect, on this twenty-four-story skyscraper in Midtown Manhattan. Mr. Portzamparc provided the building design, and Hillier served as the coordinating architect, providing design development, production documentation, and construction administration services, as well as interior architecture and design. A ground-level store for Christian Dior was designed by Peter Marino. The white-glass-mirrored tower, with a striking oblique line, is as dramatic as the fashion companies housed within its walls. The innovative structure incorporates intelligent building technologies, including fully integrated data and telecommunications systems.

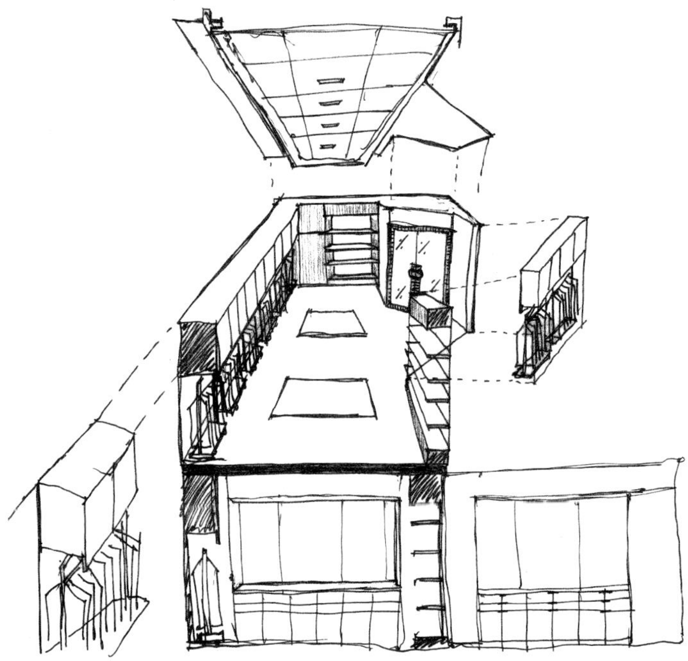

Inside the tower are offices for executives at Guerlain, Louis Vuitton, Givenchy, and several other divisions of the luxury goods conglomerate. The offices are complemented by nine showrooms and a thirty-foot-high Magic Room on the top floor—a multipurpose room used for special events, including fashion shows, product launches, and large meetings.

GlaxoSmithKline Global Headquarters

LONDON, ENGLAND
790,000 SF

Hillier's design for a global headquarters for GlaxoSmithKline, one of the world's leading research-based pharmaceutical companies, initiated a transformation within the organization and introduced a signature presence on a prominent thirteen-acre site outside of Central London at the intersection of the A4 and M4 highways.

GlaxoSmithKline

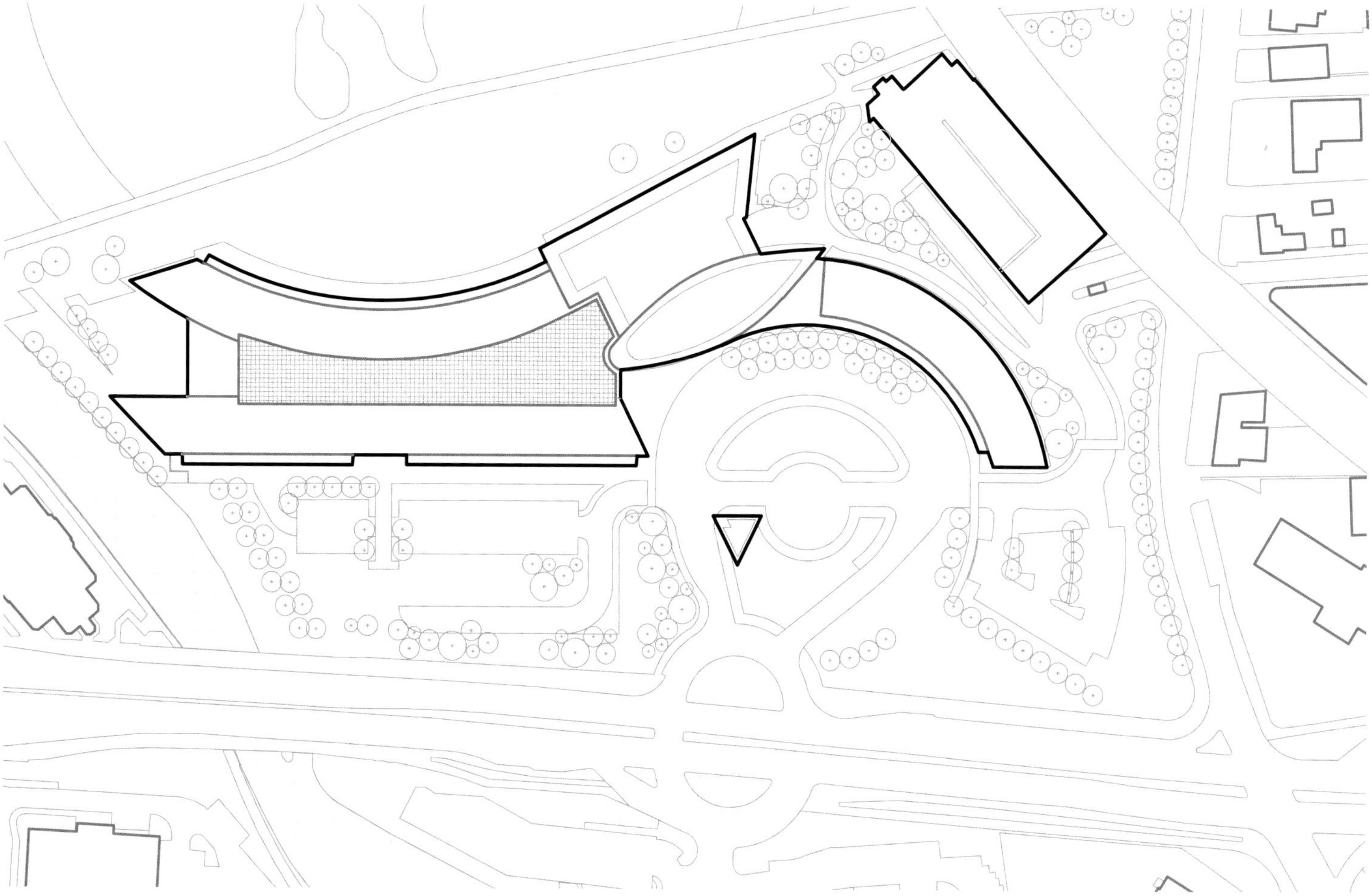

The building was designed to bring employees together in an efficient and effective work environment; to create a central space that advances GSK culture, including executive visibility and staff interaction; to create a gateway landmark that is welcoming to visitors and sensitive to the surrounding neighborhood; and to make the most of the construction budget by accelerating the design and construction process.

The headquarters for up to 3,500 people encompasses over one million square feet of space within three five-story buildings and a sixteen-story, seventy-one-meter-high glass tower. The structures are linked by a dramatic, double-curving façade of glass and natural stone fenestration. There is also a 142-meter-long interior "street," a focal point enlivened by interconnecting bridges suspended from top-level trusses that provide continuous vistas. Two aerial sculptures (next page) by British artist, Jan Blake, titled "Abundance" and "Reflex" anchor both ends of the internal street.

KiX

Howard University Stokes Library

WASHINGTON, DC
80,000 SF

The Louis Stokes Health Sciences Library creates a new campus green amid an urban morass of asphalt parking lots in Washington, DC. This new quadrangle reclaims the historic essence of Howard University's distinguished 1935 campus master plan, connecting the buildings of Howard's schools of medicine, dentistry, and nursing with the original Freedman's Hospital, our nation's first hospital for freed slaves. The library and its location reassert the university's courageous original planning that claimed and expressed the roots of American democracy. In view of Howard's Founders Library and the US Capitol Building, the Stokes Library mediates between these neoclassical monuments and today's modernity.

As one of the country's most technologically advanced centers for bioinformatics, the new Health Sciences Library houses the health sciences collections, eight problem-based computer classrooms, presentation and conference rooms, an exhibit room, distance learning labs, and a telemedicine center.

The building is organized around a four-story atrium and information commons, connecting all levels visually and spatially, flooding daylight everywhere. On the fourth floor, a barrel-vaulted reading room crowns the building and provides dramatic views of the quadrangle, campus, and city. The colonnaded west facade curves gently to focus interior reading spaces to the quadrangle and joins the octagonal tower defining the monumental entry.

ABBE SCIENCE CENTER

Solebury Abbe Science Center

SOLEBURY TOWNSHIP, PA
13,500 SF

The Hillier Group was retained to assist with the campus master plan of the Solebury School, a seventy-five-year-old private preparatory school for grades seven through twelve. The plan called for new up-to-date science classrooms and labs that would be large enough to allow research projects to remain in place for longer periods of time. Its program of four science labs with combined classrooms, four mathematics classrooms, a student lounge, and a greenhouse were to meet the highest competitive standards in pedagogy and technology, including sustainable design. The connection to the outdoors is one of the most valued aspects of the experience at Solebury and was critical to maintain.

The result is the Abbe Science Center, a one-story, L-shaped building that exploits the north-south and east-west axes for introduction of daylight and passive solar design. Long glazed hallways connecting the spaces double as student art galleries. At the elbow of the building is a two-story open area, which serves as a student study lounge and meeting space. The first modern building on the campus, the steel frame construction is exposed throughout the interior spaces. Underscoring the designer's desire to use local materials, the building is clad in a natural cedar "corn-crib," modelled after the familiar farm icon and panelized to accept ten-foot-high sliding glass patio doors.

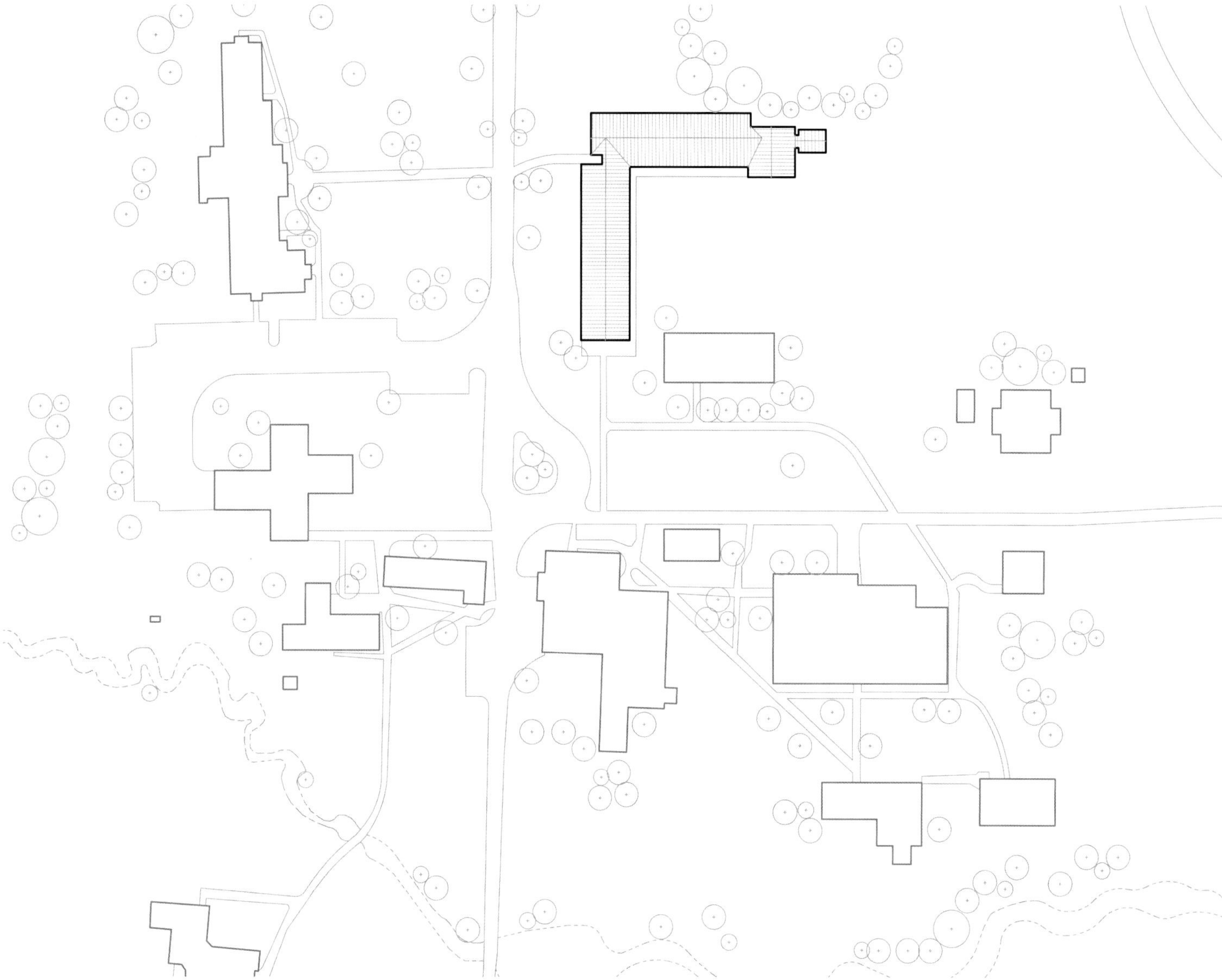

Cornell University Laboratory of Ornithology

ITHACA, NY
90,000 SF

The Cornell Laboratory of Ornithology is a 90,000-square-foot center devoted to the study, appreciation and conservation of birds and their habitats. The project includes a visitor's center and observatory, collection storage, laboratories, sound studios, the largest library of recorded bird songs in the world, and office space for the lab's extensive programs of conservation and "citizen science."

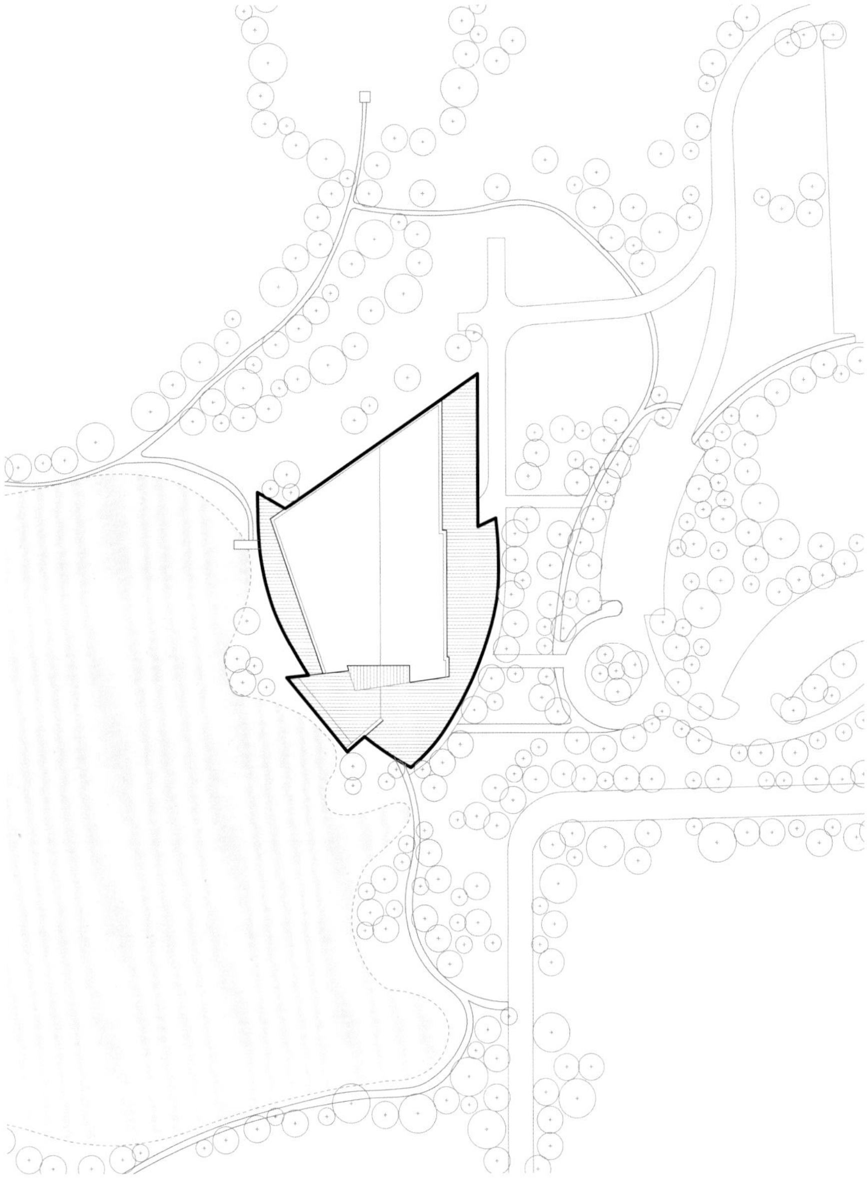

The design accommodates the extensive program for the world-famous laboratory within the wetland mosaic it created nearly forty years ago from former grazing land. Views to and from the pond, the home and inspiration of the lab, is the primary focus of the lab design for both visitors and scientists.

The architects made every effort to minimize disturbance of wetlands and keep the building in scale with its surroundings. The plans of the building as well as the location of roads, parking, and trails for the project were mapped against the existing wetlands to find the least-disruptive arrangement to the site. This generated the somewhat unusual plan configuration of the building, particularly at its north side where its diagonal shape directly follows the wetland boundary.

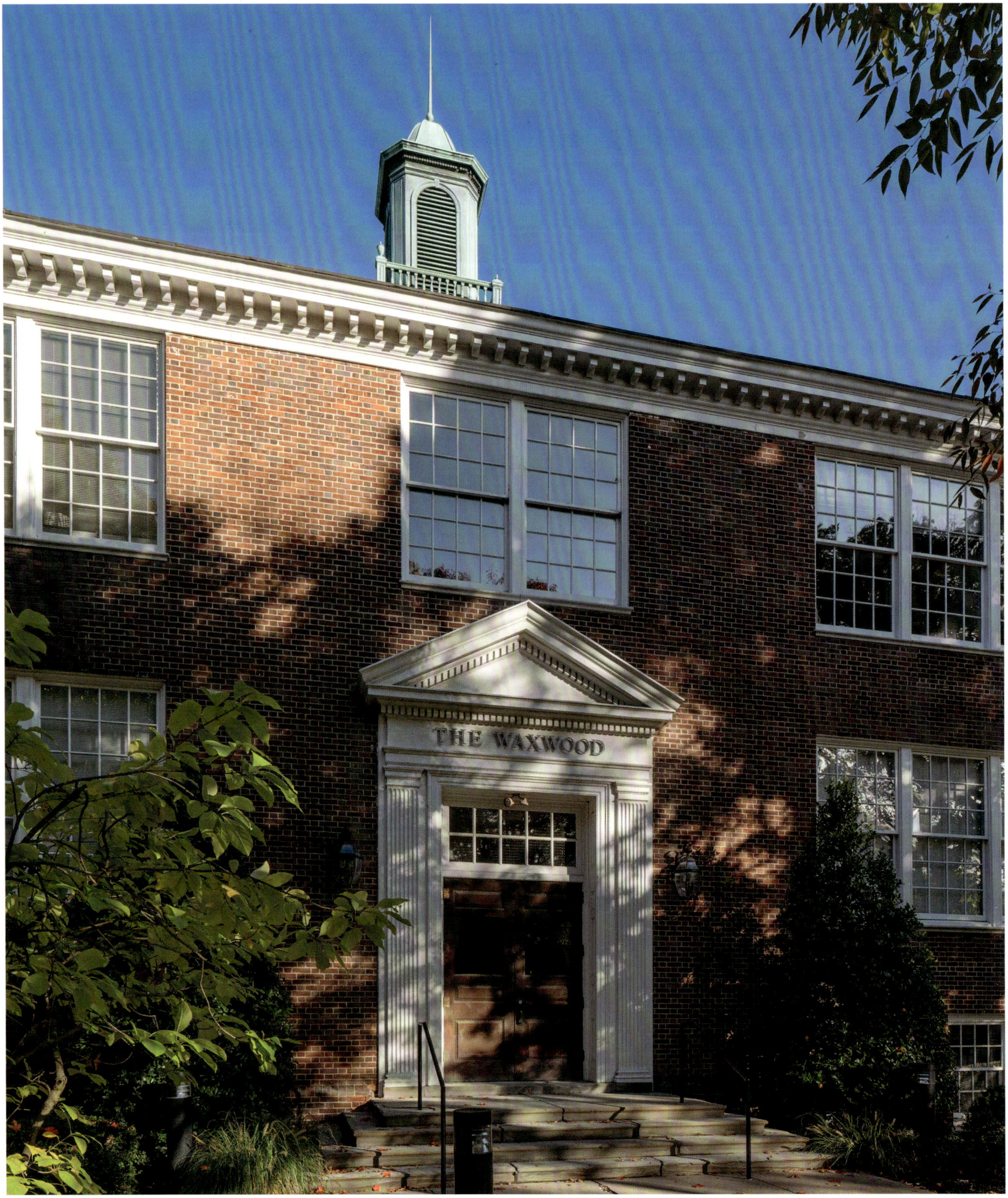
THE WAXWOOD

The Waxwood

PRINCETON, NJ
43,000 SF

Named after a well-known former principal, The Waxwood adaptively reuses the former Witherspoon School to rehabilitate a building of significant historical and cultural value and address a need for housing within Princeton Borough. The conversion of the building into thirty-four one- and two-bedroom apartments focuses on both restoring the exterior appearance to its original condition and exploring a mix of unit types, including loft apartments that frame panoramic views of the surrounding countryside.

THE WAXWOOD

Other features include a residential walking garden and a paved cobblestone entry court. Windows are restored to their full height, in some cases measuring five feet wide by over eight feet high. Totaling almost 44,000 gross square feet, the building's units range from 600 to 1,300 square feet, with several opening to private gardens or decks. All required parking is achieved on site. Two elevators serve three floors—particularly well-suited for older residents seeking to live within walking distance of downtown.

Winning the support of a primarily African American community, the project makes significant gestures to the neighborhood. Seeking to alleviate the effects of gentrification, Hillier created a foundation to assist residents in purchasing units for sale. Historical markers tell the story of the original function of the building, which served as the school for African American students prior to desegregation. Named after another venerable principal of the former school, Hillier created a pedestrian vest pocket park along Maclean Street.

House at Leeside Farm

NEW HOPE, PA
8,040 SF

Along the edge of a steeply sloping bluff overlooking the Delaware River, Hillier designed a crisp and clean single-family residence. To take advantage of the river views, the full length of the north elevation is comprised of floor-to-ceiling glass. On southern and western exposures, the home is sheltered from the sun with stone walls, deep overhangs, and a cantilevered canopy near the entry, nestled below a sod roof.

The central pavilion wraps living, dining, and kitchen areas. Sheathed with glass on all four sides, it rises on eight steel columns to a wafer-thin roof line and deep overhangs. Adjoining the pavilion on one side is a pivotal point of the residence—the greeting room. Encased in zinc, this conical room incorporates fireplace flues into its sculpted shape. Twisting outward from this space is the office and master bedroom wing, including an indoor lap pool and exercise area. Between the sloping zinc roof of the pool and the master suite is a sky-lit gallery and dressing area.

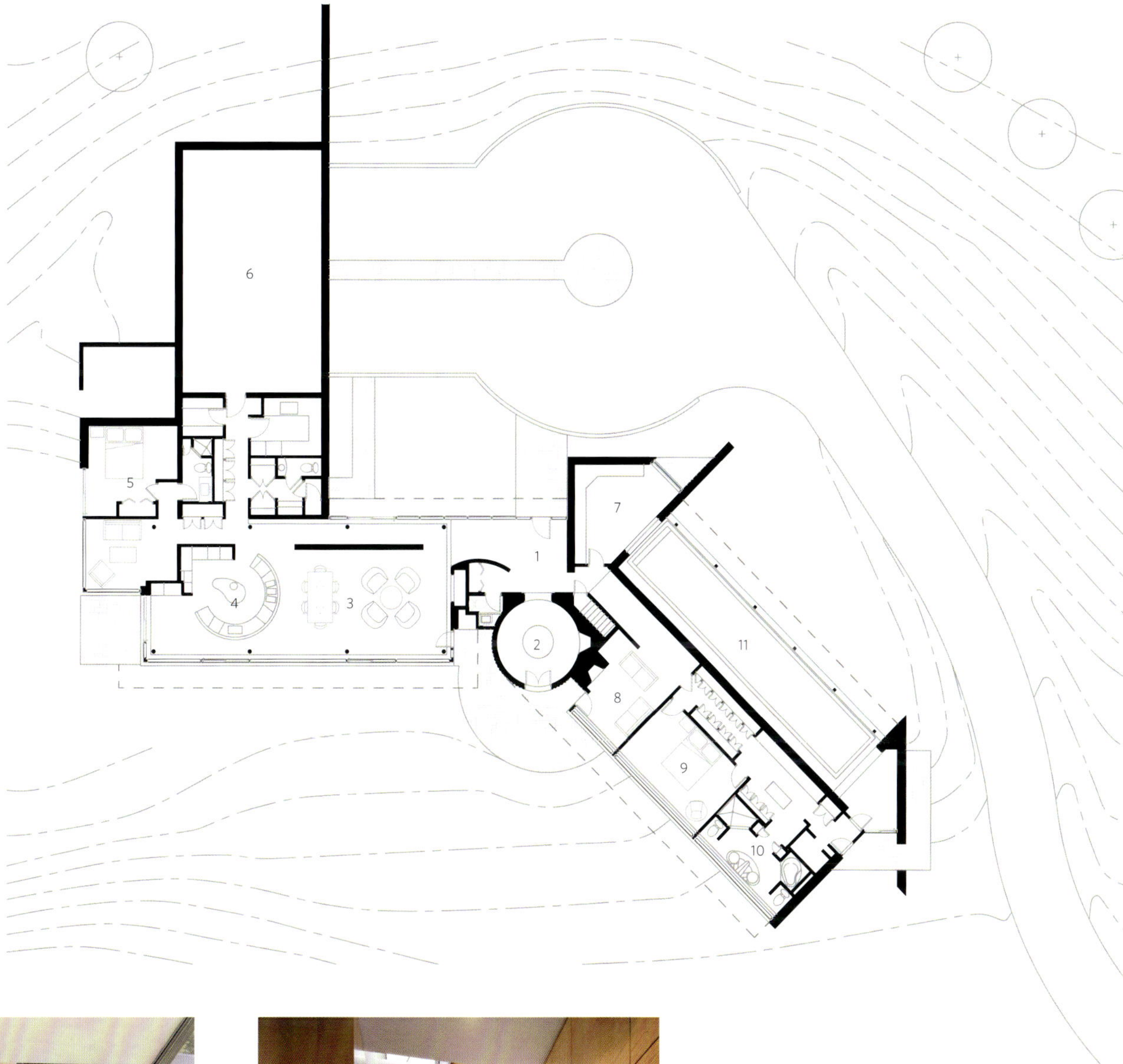

1 Entry
2 Greeting Room
3 Living/Dining
4 Kitchen
5 Guest Suite
6 Garage
7 Office
8 Master Sitting Room
9 Master Bedroom
10 Master Bathroom
11 Indoor Lap Pool

E WALTER AND LEONORE ANNENBERG SCIENCE CENTER

Peddie School Annenberg Science Center

HIGHTSTOWN, NJ
42,000 SF

The Peddie School Walter and Leonore Annenberg Science Center features teaching labs for chemistry, biology, and physics and incorporates two innovative Special Projects rooms where students explore research topics of their own choosing. The project makes an important contribution to the theory of designing school buildings with a unique central space called the "Spine of Light." This space is specifically designed to foster informal communication between teachers and students. It is a place for kids to "hang-out" with their teachers—outside a formal classroom setting. With a very large south-facing glass wall, this area is always flooded with natural light.

The architectural design of the building is dramatic, expressing the importance of science at Peddie School through the bold gesture of a sweeping curved wall of zinc and large areas of glass. To balance the bravado of the structure, the selected color palette draws from the more traditional buildings of the surrounding campus.

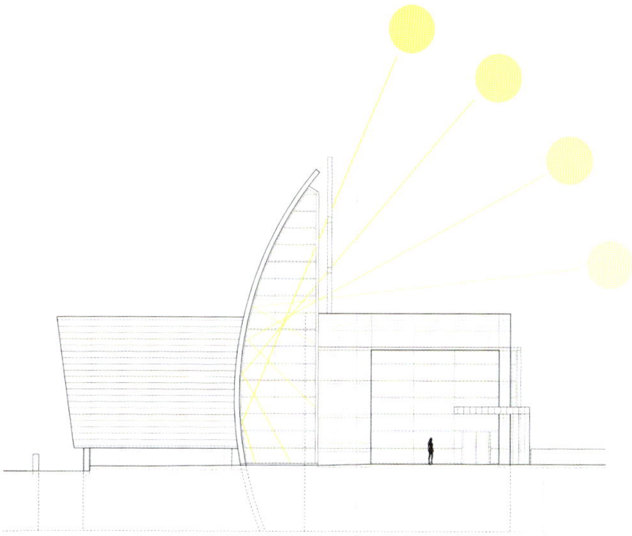

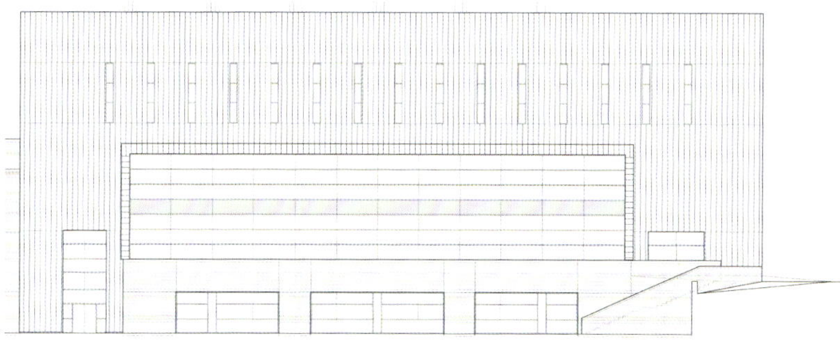

THE WALTER A

ORE ANNENBERG SCIENCE CENTER

DUKE NUS
HUMP
AHEAD
SLOW

Duke NUS Singapore

SINGAPORE
25,000 SF

Duke University Medical School and the National University of Singapore created a joint venture to develop and operate a US-style graduate medical school on the Sing Health Campus in central Singapore. Designed to enable an integrated approach combining academic learning, strong clinical training, and critical thinking skills, the ten-story building contains a variety of spaces for learning and research.

WARNING!
STOP
STOP

Fostering collaboration and creating a campus "heart" are key objectives of the central atrium. The atrium ties library and academic spaces at ground level with principal investigators and post-doctorates on the research floors above.

In keeping with local climate and tradition, the exterior's louvres and sunshades condition perimeter spaces while the building massing shades exterior spaces, making them enjoyable year-round.

AHEAD
HUMP

TUFTS

Princeton Public Library

PRINCETON, NJ
58,000 SF

Designed in concert with the diverse community it serves, the 58,000-gross-square-foot Princeton Public Library has become, in the words of its director, "a community agora for the new millennium."

Princeton Public Library
MAKING WITHERSPOON
Dineable
FIVE-STAR LIBRARY

Princeton Public Library

At three stories, the building is both monumental in scale and openly welcoming. A large glass "porch" and playful glass staircase create a lively "see and be seen" theatricality along the main street, while quiet spaces and reading nooks are secluded throughout the building. Materials are attractively "merchandised" through custom displays, lighting and graphics forming interior landscapes that invite browsing and inspire exploration for every level of user. Children are uniquely given "pride of place" on the third floor, including a tower room, story center, and their own special outdoor garden terrace.

Sprinkled throughout the "all wi-fi" building's public spaces—which include a large community room, café, two working fireplaces, a technology center, and a variety of meeting and lounging spaces—the library exhibits breathtaking artwork by world-class artists that was especially commissioned for the building. The Princeton Public Library has become the heart of downtown Princeton, fulfilling the vision of civic leaders, city residents, architects, and the library staff.

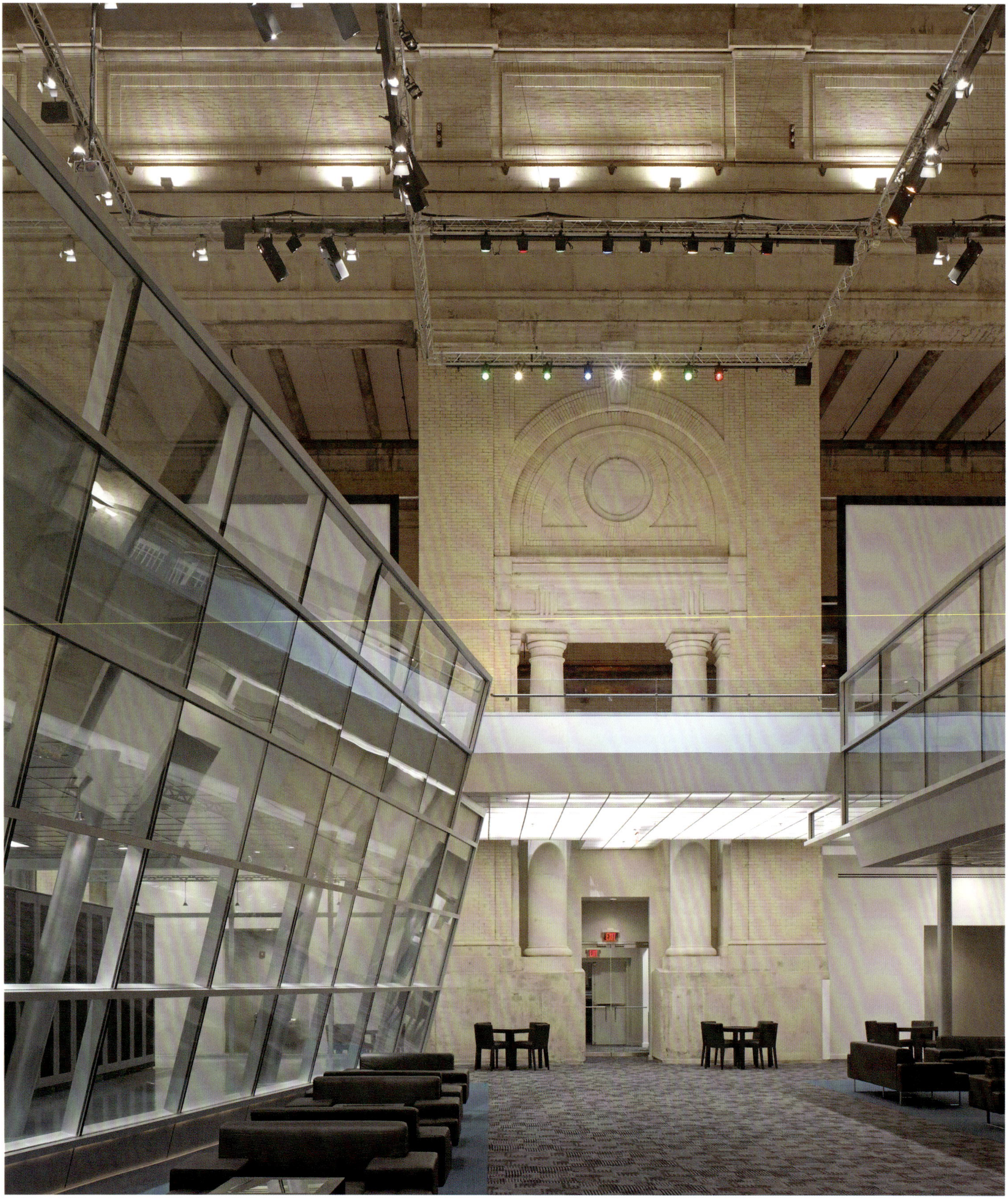

Synygy World Headquarters

CHESTER, PA
130,000 SF

Synygy selected Hillier to transform a massive industrial-age power station into Synygy's new world headquarters. The award-winning project helped the company set the benchmark for industry leadership, corporate responsibility, and community involvement. Named the "Best Adaptive Reuse Project of the Year" in 2006 by the International Design Association, Philadelphia City Center Chapter, Hillier's transformation of the aging power station was also honored by the Philadelphia Preservation Alliance and received the 2006 Commonwealth Design Award from 10,000 Friends of Pennsylvania.

The original power station was a monument to the production and marketing of electricity in the early 20th century, featuring advances in power generation and industrial construction. Accommodating modern technology and enabling a design that would facilitate future growth first required the removal of much of the equipment from the past. The old Turbine Hall, with its 100-foot vaulted ceiling, now houses two new freestanding structures, incorporating a data center, cafeteria, and conference center. The roofs of these structures serve as a plaza, an open patio, and a multi-functional theater/trade show area.

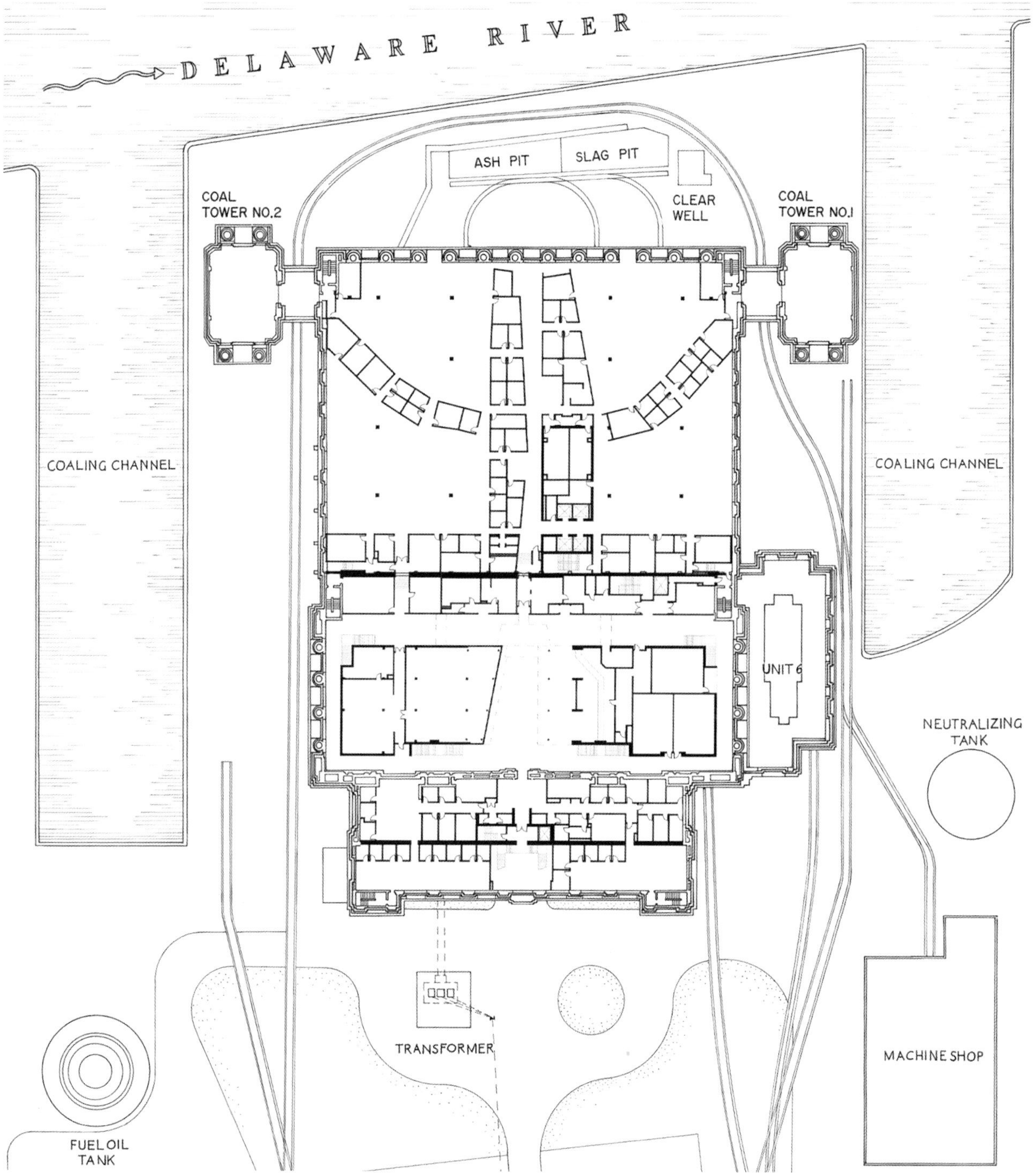
DELAWARE RIVER
ASH PIT
SLAG PIT
COAL TOWER NO.2
CLEAR WELL
COAL TOWER NO.1
COALING CHANNEL
COALING CHANNEL
UNIT 6
NEUTRALIZING TANK
TRANSFORMER
MACHINE SHOP
FUEL OIL TANK

New Jersey Medical School Cancer Center

NEWARK, NJ
214,000 SF

The University of Medicine and Dentistry of New Jersey (now part of Rutgers University) retained Hillier to design a new 214,000-square-foot, state-of-the-art comprehensive Cancer Center in Newark. The Cancer Center includes research, clinical, administrative, and support spaces. The research space includes wet laboratories, lab support space, and vivarium. This facility incorporates the latest in technological research approaches with flexible and efficient laboratory work space and houses outpatient treatment areas for cancer patients, as well as sophisticated cancer research laboratories. It is the intent of the design to have cancer research on display, assuring patients that future cures and current treatments are integrated in one building.

The Cancer Center complements its surrounding area while creating a strong presence at the perimeter of the campus. This location provides convenient access to existing radiation oncology, animal research, and medical education facilities. Hillier assisted UMDNJ in successfully applying for and receiving millions of dollars for research space funding from the National Institutes of Health.

The building's striking exterior wraps an interior focused on patient experience and amenities including a community education resource center and healing garden. An open atrium infuses healing and research spaces throughout the building with copious daylight.

Duke University French Science Center

DURHAM, NC
275,000 SF

The French Science Center includes 275,000 square feet of teaching and research space for the Biology, Chemistry, and Physics Departments. The building contains state-of-the-art research and collections, greenhouses, and connects with the existing Biology and Physics Buildings to strengthen the research community on campus. To help unify the research buildings, the project includes significant landscape and utility improvements as well as selected renovations in the existing facilities.

The modular design incorporates a combination of bench research, laboratory support, and shared support in laboratory spaces. The design of casework and services easily facilitates changing team size, new equipment, and research needs. Locating faculty and graduate offices adjacent to the laboratories provides easy access and communication.

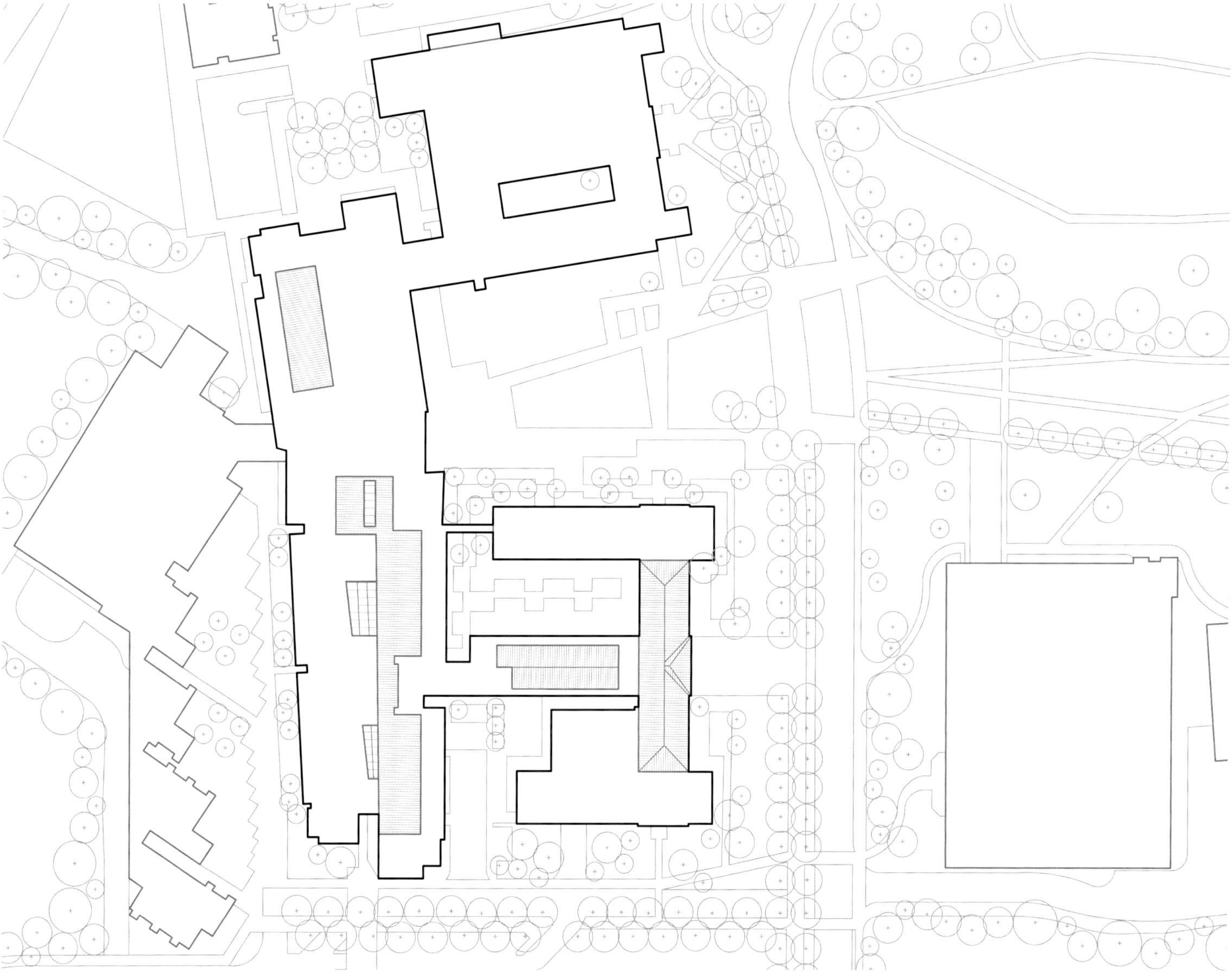

The design centers research, teaching, office, and support spaces around an atrium, the vertical connection for the building's various functions. The atrium extends daylight into the building and provides a link to the adjacent research buildings. Communal spaces are located throughout the atrium to encourage interaction.

Central Park North

NEW YORK, NY
150,00 SF

The project's greatest challenge was constructing a building in the architecturally prescriptive city of New York. Understanding the building's constraints drove extensive research into design solutions. The envelope satisfies certain civic obligations while simultaneously honoring the project's location as a gateway into Harlem.

Overlooking Central Park's Harlem Meer, the residential tower contains approximately ninety-five apartments over a commercial ground floor and includes a 4,500-square-foot community facility for the neighborhood and parking. The plan carefully integrates the design into the surrounding fabric of the neighborhood and Central Park. At the urban scale, the beacon-like tower heralds the community across the greater cityscape.

Timeline

Timeline

1963

After completing his graduate studies at Princeton under Jean Labatut, Bob serves as the designer/drafter for the Labatut-designed Stuart Country Day School in Princeton.

1966

On April 1, J. Robert Hillier leases his first office at 44 Nassau Street in Princeton, NJ. Bob's first job was replacing a bathroom vanity for a wealthy Princeton client, which soon evolved into a commission to renovate their corporate office building in Chicago.

1967

Bob designs a three-story office building, a dormitory for Fairleigh Dickinson University, and a private residence, all three of which win AIA design awards from the New Jersey Society of Architects.

Residence of Mr. and Mrs. Large

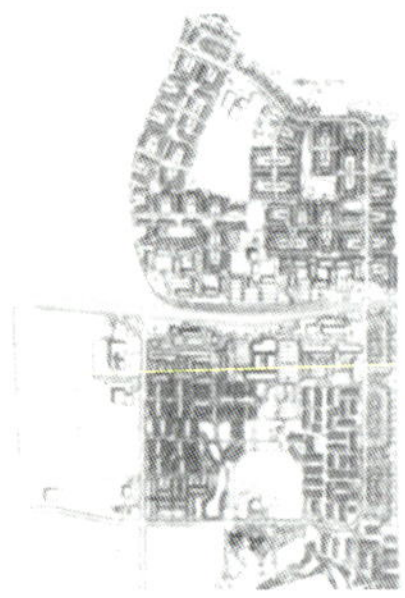

1969

Twin Rivers is the first planned unit development (PUD) in New Jersey, with over 700 townhouses near enough to one another for residents to walk to work, shopping, and entertainment, a concept prohibited by prevailing zoning restrictions at the time.

1970

The business expands to forty-eight employees and moves to a building at the end of Princeton Airport's runway that a plane had once crashed into.

Bryant University Unistructure

1973

Now recognized as a professional corporation, J. Robert Hillier, Architects, PA moves into its own building known as the "*Treehouse*," the first building in New Jersey approved to be designed and built in a floodplain.

The Treehouse

1974

Decades before sustainable design was at the forefront of architectural practice, Hillier emphasizes land use and energy strategies to create environmentally responsible buildings. Their first international project, the *American International School in Vienna*, is completed. This is the first of twelve international secondary schools designed by Hillier.

1975

Engineering News-Record ranks Hillier as no. 308 of 500 top design firms in the United States based on revenue and size.

1976

Barbara Weinstein creates and leads the Interiors Studio. J. Robert Hillier is elected to the AIA College of Fellows.

1977

The first passive solar-heated municipal building in New Jersey, designed for East Windsor, is profiled by the *New York Times*. Environmental strategies include a Trombe wall, sod roof, and sophisticated interior light controls.

1978

Beneficial Management, Inc., commissions a new 500,000-square-foot corporate headquarters in Peapack, NJ. This pioneering headquarters would lead to further commissions for corporate campuses from some of the world's largest corporations.

1980

The firm hires its one hundredth employee and becomes The Hillier Group, Architects/ Planners, PA.

1981

Now the ninth largest architectural firm in the nation, the firm moves into the building known as the "*Solar Wedge*."

1982

The *Richard J. Hughes Justice Complex* in Trenton, NJ, was one of the largest projects ever undertaken by the state of New Jersey at the time of its completion.

1984

Hillier opens an office in Tampa, FL, to design and support the development of *Harbour Island* and is named New Jersey's Firm of the Year by the Business and Industry Association.

1985

On the tenth Hillier "Career Day," Bob invites 100 aspiring architects to spend a day at the firm. 17 "Career Day" participants will eventually become Hillier employees.

1986

In need of more office space, The Hillier Group moves to a new headquarters at *500 Alexander Park* and celebrates their twentieth anniversary.

1987

The Hillier Group wins a national competition to design an addition to *Arizona State University's College of Architecture and Environmental Design.*

1987

The Hillier Group is the country's seventh largest architectural firm with a staff of 235, having executed over 2,000 projects for 700 clients.

1988

Under the leadership of Design and Managing Principal Barbara Hillier, a full-service regional office opens in Philadelphia.

1989

Inc. Magazine names J. Robert Hillier as New Jersey's "Entrepreneur of the Year," and Hillier publishes *"Ten Ways of Looking at a Building: A Guide to the Rights of Clients."*

1990

With technological advancements, Hillier's first website launches under the direction of chief spec writer Marty Bloomenthal, later chair of AIA National Specification Committee. The firm implements CAD across all offices.

1993

Architectural Record profiles Hillier's design for the *AT&T Corporate Campus* in Bridgewater, NJ, an early example of green architecture.

1993

The Hillier Group acquires GSGSB Architects, Engineers, Planners of Clarks Summit, PA, expanding their market to new areas, such as data centers.

Vanguard Corporate Headquarters

1994

Part of a strategic plan to provide full design services locally and regionally, the Eggers Group is acquired, and a New York office is formed, now one of eight locations.

Cancer Specialists of Georgia

1994

Star City Sydney Harbour Mixed-Use Development revitalizes the historic Pyrmont Bay waterfront in Sydney, Australia.

1995

The result of an initiative to consolidate research operations, the new one-million-square-foot *SmithKlineBeecham* Research Center is one of England's largest capital projects.

1996

Celebrating theirthirtieth anniversary, Hillier rebrands and launches a new logo.

1996

The *Cogeneration Plant at John F. Kennedy International Airport in New York* wins accolades and recognition, including a profile in the *Wall Street Journal*.

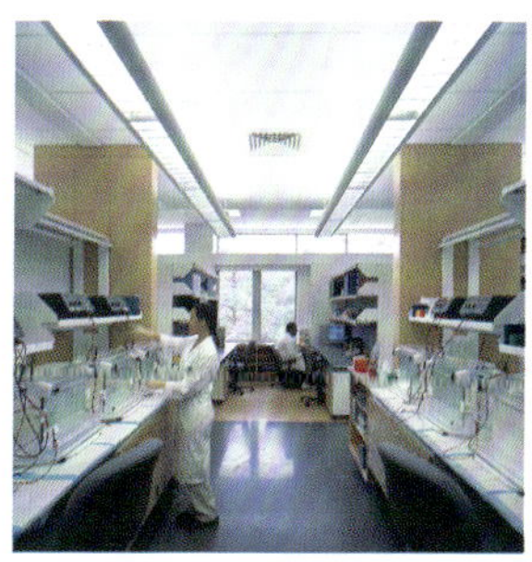

1997

At the *Duke University Center for Human Genomics*, an international leader in the study of inherited disorders, futuristic laboratories provide ideal spaces for scientists dedicating their time to genetic discoveries.

1998

Architectural Record features Hillier as one of the best-managed firms in the United States. A new Hillier website is launched.

1999

Looking to reclaim its position as Newark's Crown Jewel, the outdated *National Newark Building* is cleaned and transformed, inside and out.

2000

Hillier completes the design for *Turkiye Is Bankasi Headquarters* in Istanbul.

2000

The revolutionary *Niagara Falls High School* is featured in the *New York Times*.

2001

Hillier completes the five-million-square-foot *Sprint Headquarters Campus* in Overland Park, KS.

2002

GlaxoSmithKline Global Headquarters in London, UK, symbolizes the company's forward position as one of the world's leading pharmaceutical companies.

2003

Capital One Corporate Campus in Richmond, VA, comprises nine buildings in groups of three, each joined by "knuckle" components containing amenity and support spaces.

2004

Hillier opens an office in Shanghai and launches an award-winning website that is people-centric, not just project-focused.

2004

The *Solebury School Abbe Science Center* receives the AIA Pennsylvania Silver Medal, the state's most prestigious award representing the highest level of achievement in design.

2005

Engineering News-Record ranks Hillier fifth of the top one hundred "pure" architecture firms in the United States, and the firm wins fourteen design awards.

Peddie School Annenberg Science Center

2006

Hillier Architecture is named AIA New Jersey Architectural Firm of the Year.

2007

J. Robert Hillier receives the Michael Graves Lifetime Achievement Award from AIA NJ. In receiving the chapter's most prestigious award, Bob is only the second architect to earn this award for "completion of a significant architectural body of work and the influence it has had on the practice of architecture."

2008

The *Becton Dickinson Corporate Campus Employee Services Center* wins the American Architecture Award from the Chicago Athenaeum.

2009

Bob personally designs the chapel at the *Penn Medicine Princeton Medical Center*, a project completed in collaboration with HOK.

2012

Bob and Barbara establish Studio Hillier in downtown Princeton, renewing their focus on smaller scale, local and community projects.

2013

Studio Hillier designs, develops, and operates *Copperwood*, a 153-unit residential development in Princeton.

2014

The work of Hillier Architecture is featured at the US Pavilion of the Venice Biennale.

2015

Studio Hillier is featured in "The Built Environment: Design for Life" exhibit by the Trenton City Museum at Ellarslie.

The Lawrenceville School Kirby Math and Science Center

2016

J. Robert Hillier celebrates fifty years of architecture.

Iona University Residence Hall

2017

New townhouses for the *Institute for Advanced Study* provide a natural extension of the institute's existing campus while allowing a significant expansion of preserved land for Princeton Battlefield State Park.

2018

Studio Hillier is named Design Architect for *Port St. George*, a net zero-carbon resort in the Bahamas.

2019

New Jersey Institute of Technology (NJIT) renames its architecture and design school the J. Robert and Barbara A. Hillier College of Architecture and Design.

2020

At the outset of the pandemic, Studio Hillier fabricates and donates 2,800 3D-printed face shields to healthcare workers and opens its office as a free food-distribution center.

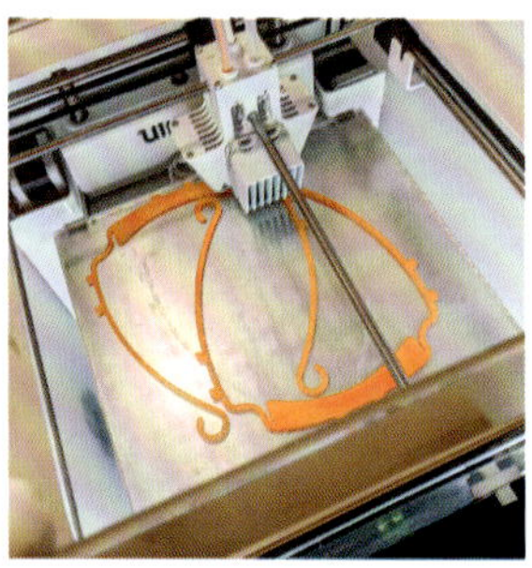

2021

The *Cove at Manhattan Beach*, a 500-unit multifamily development facing Raritan Bay, is notable for its creation of a new living shoreline with a tidal marsh on a remediated brownfield site.

2022

In November 2022, Barbara A. Hillier, AIA, passed away after fighting Alzheimer's disease. Over 500 family members, friends, past and present colleagues attended the celebration of her life.

PRESENT

Today, Studio Hillier is building on our legacy of success and client satisfaction while delivering future-focused design incorporating the latest building technologies, environmental systems, and preservation of historic structures.

Quarry Street Two-Plex

PRINCETON, NJ
TWO UNITS

This duplex house replaces a derelict structure on a tree-lined street in the relatively dense John Witherspoon neighborhood of Princeton Borough, a short walk from Princeton University and the very active center of town.

A modern insertion on an architecturally eclectic street, the structure maintains the scale and rhythm of the neighborhood. The selection of materials, in particular the polycarbonate siding, brings a sparkle and energy to the streetscape.

Inside, each home features a one-and-a-half-story living room, an elevator serving every level, and a central stair lit by a clerestory. Each unit has a private south-facing lawn. Outside, a white painted brick topped by polycarbonate panels sheaths one side of the duplex, while black porcelain tile with custom zinc siding covers the other unit. The residence was built in complete conformance with local zoning code. The architect for the property is also its developer.

Known as "Urban Insertion," this duplex housing project was awarded the top honor for Design Excellence by AIA (American Institute of Architects) New Jersey and the Builder's Choice Merit Award.

Becton Dickinson Campus Center

FRANKLIN LAKES, NJ
35,000 SF

The chosen site for the campus center on the Becton Dickinson corporate campus was the prominent ceremonial lawn framed by the two massive masonry office buildings. The CEO imagined a new campus center as the virtual knot that would join the two stand-alone office buildings and unify the campus's executive management and technical staff, becoming the symbol of a new, unified collaborative workforce. The campus center facility bridges and blurs the boundaries between building/landscape, indoor/outdoor, roof/earth, and the two local business cultures of management/production.

Sustainable design was elemental in both the campus center's design, which features a vegetative roof, and the site design. The reconstituted lawn reduces storm water run-off and minimizes below-grade structures and piping and eliminates heat islands.

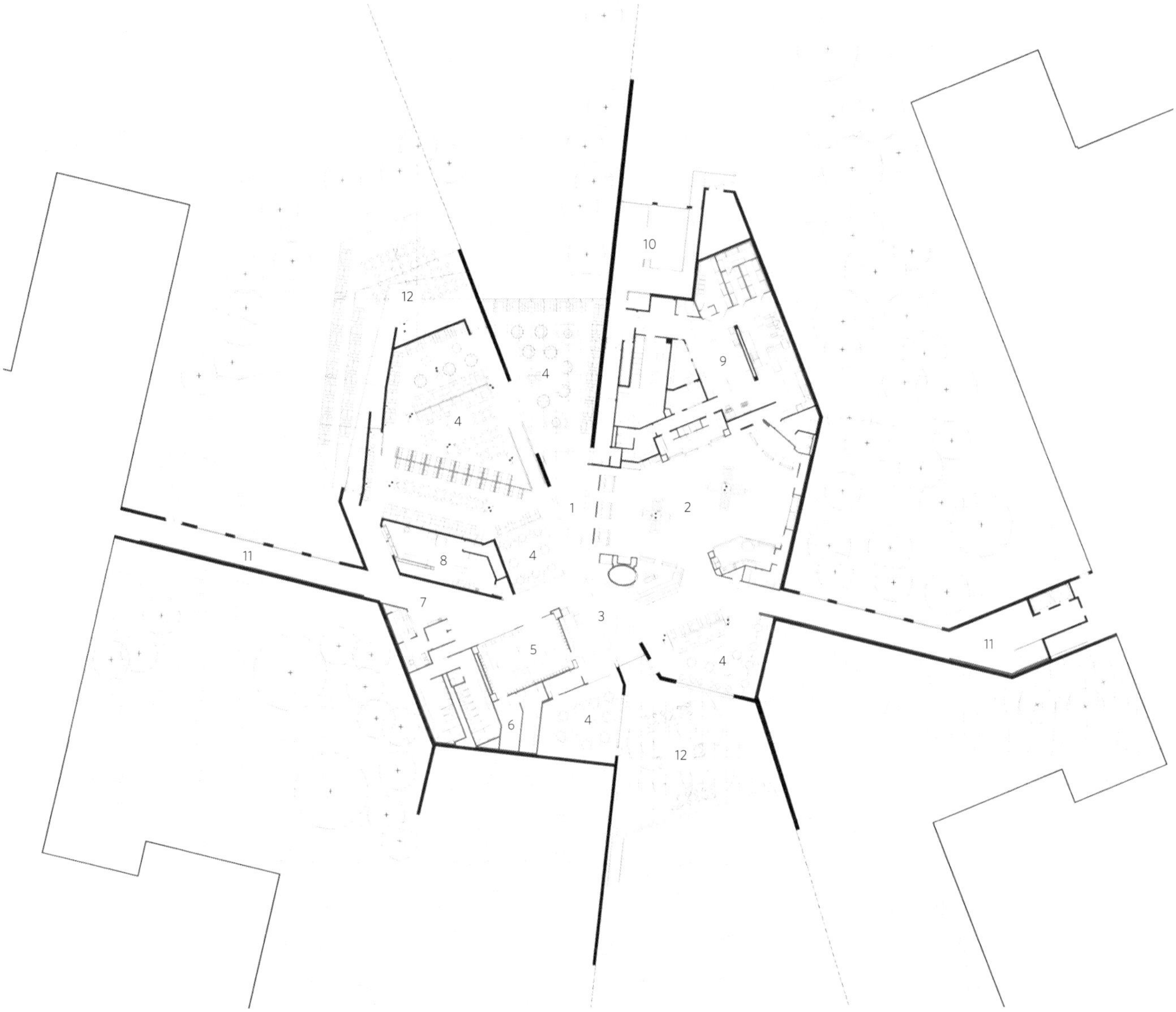

1 Intersection
2 Servery
3 Café
4 Dining
5 Retail
6 Dry Cleaner
7 Bank
8 Dish Return
9 Kitchen
10 Loading
11 Connector
12 Terrace Dining

EXIT

Goucher College Athenaeum

BALTIMORE, MD
70,000 SF

The Athenaeum at Goucher College combines the energies, talents and traditions of its campus and community in one central location. Anchored by a new, technologically superior library, the signature building serves as both a physical centerpiece for the campus and the figurative heart of its academic community. The new library expands the college's collection capacity by 50,000 volumes, for a total of approximately 350,000, and will be fully wired with state-of-the-art technology.

EXIT

Elevator
Restrooms
Commons

Outside the library's doors, a spacious open forum—modeled after the amphitheaters of Europe—serves as a focal point for outdoor events and performances. The character of this wide-open space changes from day-to-day and even hour-by-hour. The lower level is a stage that can be configured to accommodate various kinds of readings, performances, panel discussions and other public events. A giant video screen serves as its backdrop.

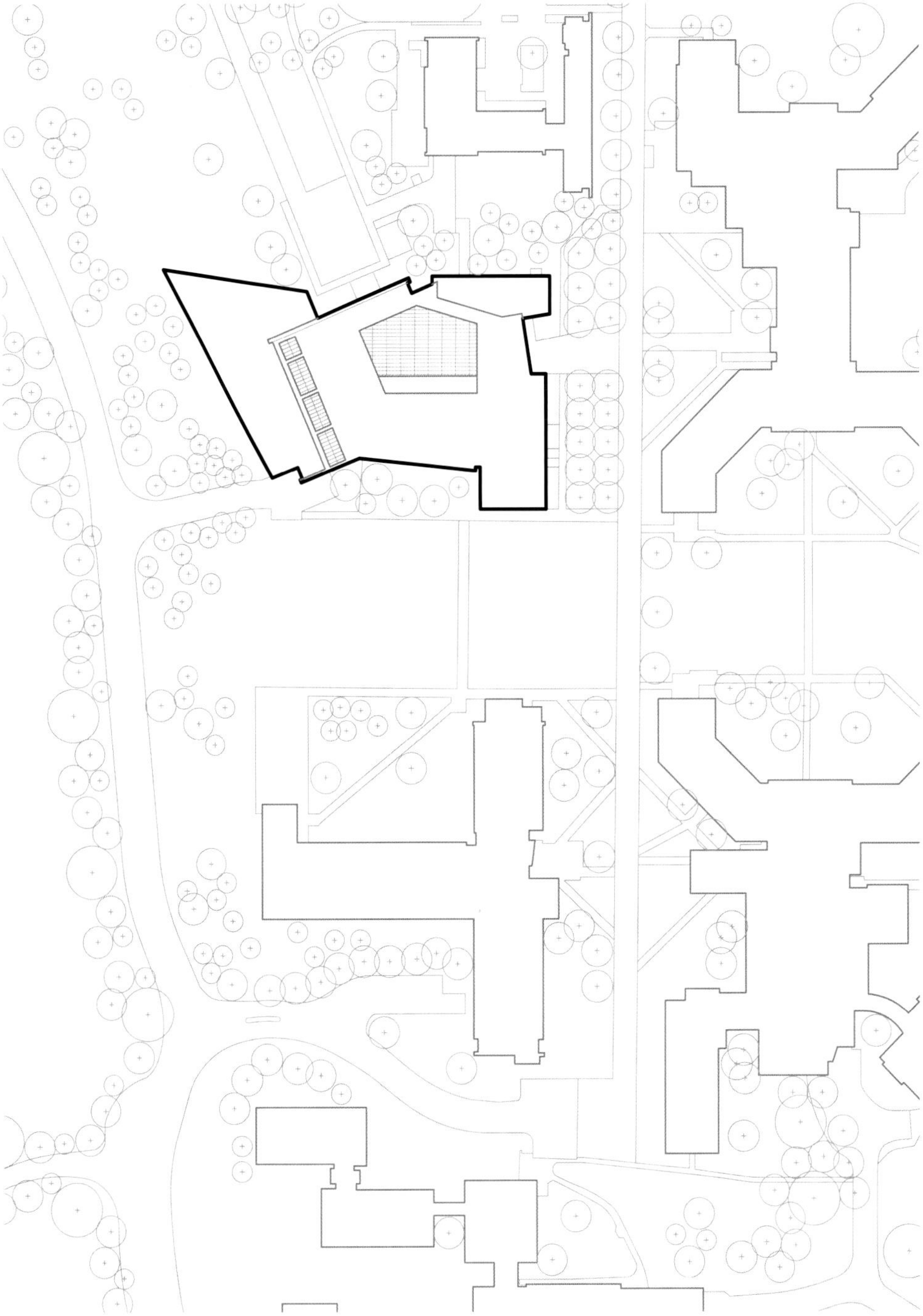

These central elements connect to a café, art gallery, college radio station, and center for the college's community service and multicultural affairs programming, as well as space for exercise, conversation, and quiet reflection and relaxation.

As part of Goucher's mission to be a "green" campus, the athenaeum incorporates several sustainable design features including a green roof, a rain garden, high-performance glass, recycled materials, and efficient mechanical systems.

Inspired by the modernist, crafted aesthetic for which the Goucher campus is increasingly well-known, the exterior includes elements of glass, stone, wood, and copper—the predominant materials found in Goucher's buildings.

Irving Convention Center

IRVING, TX
275,000 SF

With few exceptions, the north Texas landscape is flat, hot, and braided by massive concrete highways. Caught in the vortex is Las Colinas, a 12,000-acre mixed-use development, where one enters their office though a darkened garage and glides from auto to elevator without so much as a whiff of grass cuttings. Sidewalks are scarce to nonexistent, proof that architecture has the irreducible capacity to cleave the human population from nature.

Parking Garage
P
Guest & Car Drop-Off

IRVING
CONVENTION
CENTER
AT LAS COLINAS
500

The convention center is a counter proposal to the culture of containment that has proliferated in the Dallas-Fort Worth Metroplex. Convention goers and meeting attendees discover the antidote in the nonprogrammed space that constructs a set of outdoor experiences in the form of ramps, stairs, and expansive roof terraces en plein air. The stramp (stair ramp) opens a dialogue of free and independent movement that we associate with civic space. These unprogrammed spaces invite the chance, spontaneous encounters where people are most likely to engage each other.

The project is LEED certified for its integration of sustainable principles and generative design.

190
studiohillier
architecture | urban planning | design

Urban Trifecta

PRINCETON, NJ
10,000 SF

Studio Hillier identified an opportunity to transform a warehouse/garage on Witherspoon Street in downtown Princeton into a storefront architectural studio. The studio is flanked on either side by a residential-turned-commercial property that was also in need of revitalization. By restoring life into the buildings and the street, Studio Hillier sought to further enhance the surrounding neighborhood and community.

B+B HAIR COLOR STUDIO
190

190
190
190
FDC

The comprehensive plan to integrate retail, residential and office space was developed through several meetings with the Witherspoon-Jackson Community. By engaging with local residents and community leaders from the beginning of the design process, valuable and helpful information was offered and incorporated into the design.

In addition to the 6,600-square-foot warehouse transformation into an architectural studio, the two adjacent properties were turned into 2,000 square feet of retail on the ground floor and 2,000 square feet of residential space above. Four apartment units were created, two of which meet the affordable housing requirements.

1 Unit A
2 Unit B
3 Unit C
4 Unit D
5 Retail
6 Commercial

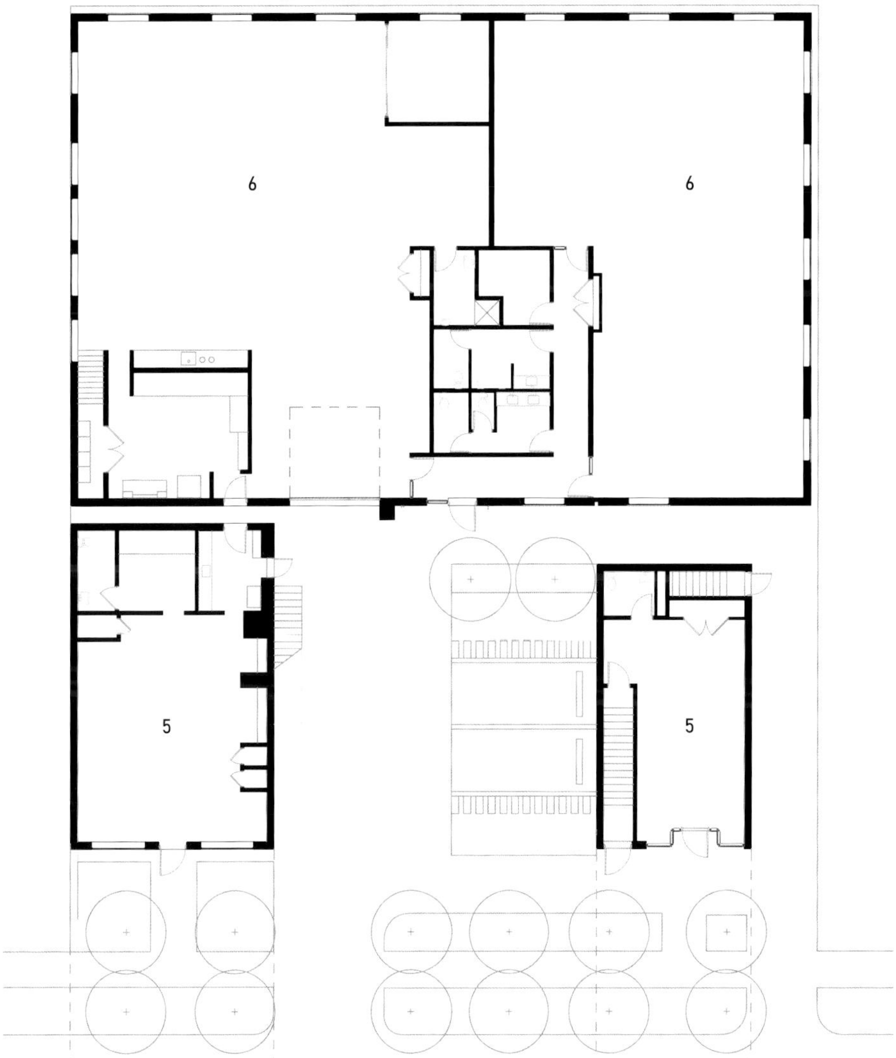

GROUND FLOOR PLAN

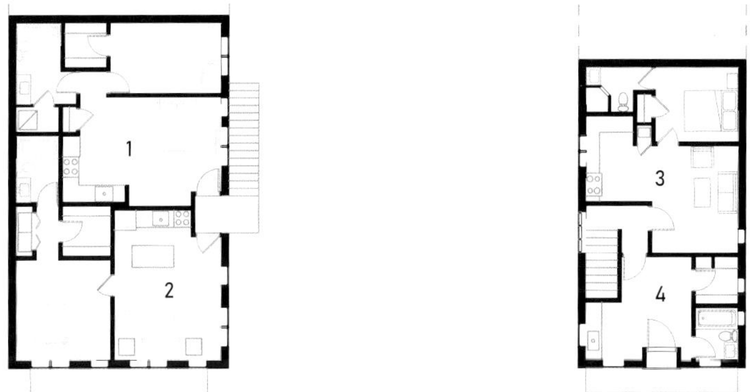

SECOND FLOOR PLAN

Penn Medicine Princeton Medical Center

PLAINSBORO, NJ
611,000 SF

Penn Medicine Princeton Medical Center, formerly known as the University Medical Center of Princeton at Plainsboro (UMCPP), is a 355-bed, nonprofit, acute-care hospital. Though often perceived as a community hospital, its services extend regionally. Hillier Architecture provided feasibility studies for UMCPP's relocation onto a new green-field site.

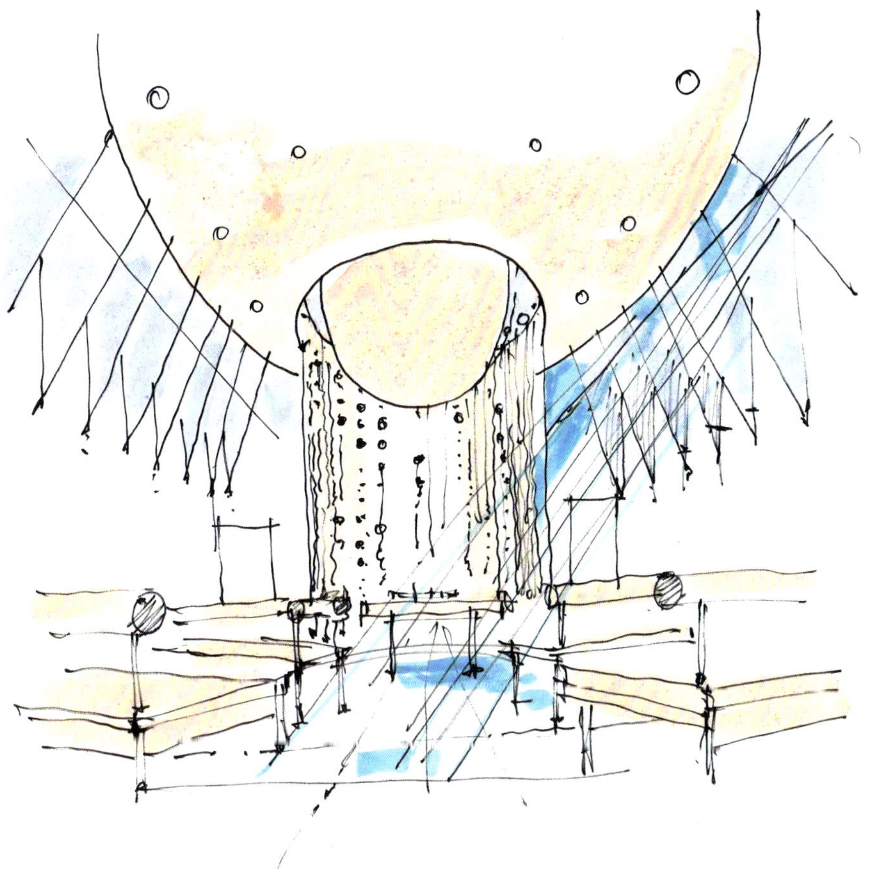

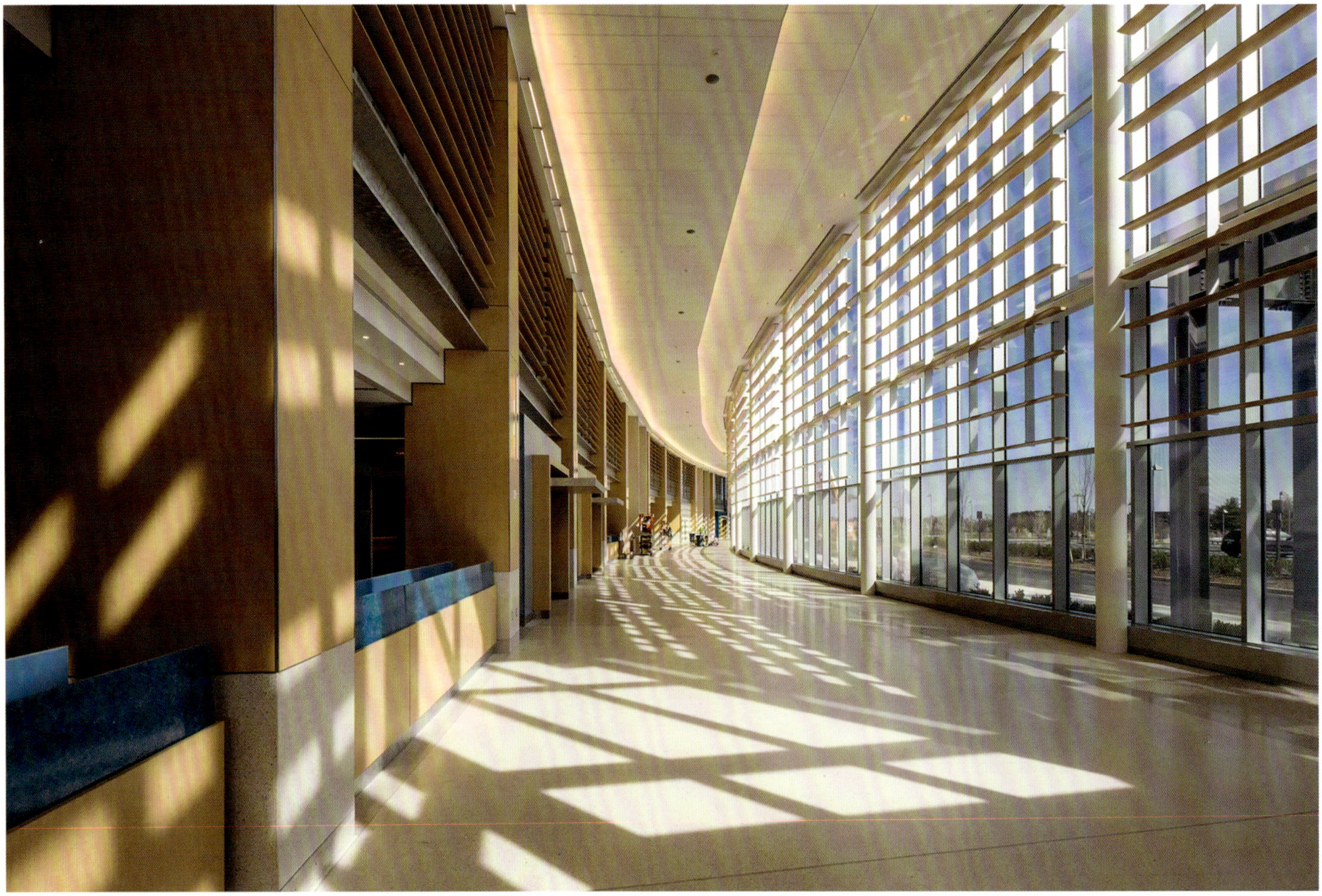

Evidence-based design, which links the quality of the hospital environment to patient healing and recovery rates, is at the heart of the design for the new hospital. From the abundant, natural light to spacious and flexible operating rooms to all-private patient rooms designed to reduce falls and minimize the risk of infection, every aspect of the hospital's design conveys a healing and welcoming atmosphere for patients, their families, and hospital staff.

The hospital's sustainable design includes many energy and conservation innovations to make it one of the most environmentally advanced hospitals in the nation. To maximize the use of natural light while controlling solar heat gain, the building is configured is on an east-west orientation relative to the site. On the façade, a sunlight-regulating exterior screen significantly reduces the amount of energy required for heating and cooling.

Additional features include a chilled water thermal storage system and environmental controls for lighting and temperature; the site's landscaping also features indigenous plants.

7189

Solebury Two-Plex

NEW HOPE, PA
TWO UNITS

The existing foundations of a hundred-year-old derelict duplex on a site forbidden by modern zoning and within stream buffers disallowed by environmental constraints served as the platform on which to build a new structure of two housing units. It is called a "two-plex" because each unit is distinctly different.

SPEED LIMIT
25
NO THRU TRAFFIC

The fenestration and siding arrangements break down the mass of the building while maintaining the verticality of the original building.

In each unit, a bedroom was sacrificed to give a two-story height to the living rooms. The indoor and outdoor living areas of each unit front onto the stream. The south unit also has an elevated deck patio, part of which is a green roof.

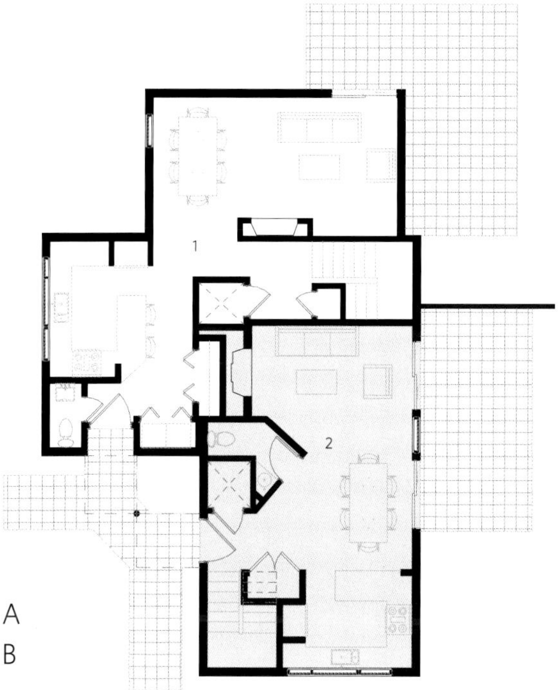

1 Unit A
2 Unit B

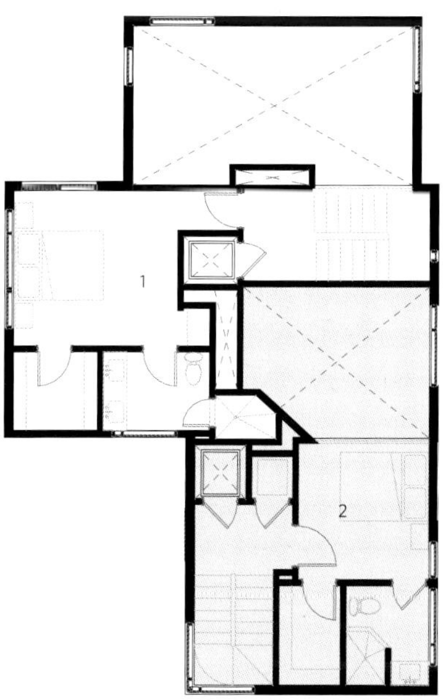

1 Unit A
2 Unit B

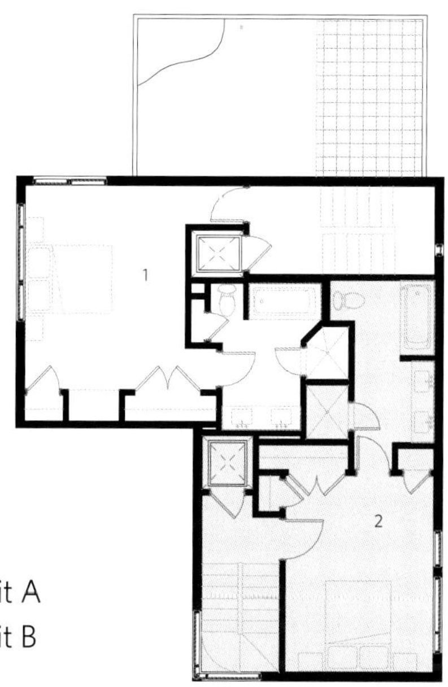

1 Unit A
2 Unit B

Copperwood

PRINCETON, NJ
153 UNITS

Copperwood is a 153-unit rental apartment complex on a beautifully wooded site in Princeton Township, surrounded by the 200-acre Princeton Ridge Preserve. Natural, muted colors and materials conceal the exterior of the complex in the woods, and the sunlit interior courtyards are enlivened with a hint of light yellow. This coloration has been implemented to respect the character of Princeton Ridge Preserve. We believe that the context of the site is as important as the building proposed. More than seventeen acres of the twenty-one-acre site was preserved as dedicated public open space giving the residents unobstructed views of the natural setting in all directions. (This site design actually saved 487 trees more than a previously approved design by a national homebuilder and disturbed only 17 percent of the site versus the original 77 percent.)

Copperwood is sited on a twenty-one-acre site on a gently sloping ground adjacent to the public Hilltop Park. In order to preserve the site with its pristine beech tree landscape, the project footprint was minimized with five apartment buildings tightly organized around piazzas, courtyards, and gardens sitting atop a garage. The careful placement of the complex into the existing woods has minimized the site disturbance and tree removal.

East River Science Park

NEW YORK, NY
870,000 SF

The East River Science Park, an 870,000-square-foot state-of-the-art science complex on Manhattan's East Side, aims to boost New York City's biotech industry and create a thriving intellectual and social space with spectacular views of the East River waterfront. The design reflects the idea that some of the most successful working environments are characterized by cooperation, the active exchange of ideas, and respect for their surroundings. A variety of spaces, some busy and active, others ideal for quiet introspection, all designed to encourage scientific breakthroughs. The interconnectivity of public and private is a key component of this striking design.

JOAN AND JOEL SMILOW RESEARCH CENTER

The western portion of the Science Park is organized around Twenty-Ninth Street, which is realigned to the Manhattan grid and opened to both cars and pedestrians. The street culminates in a new central piazza—the heart of the science campus, in the center of three research facilities. Just south of the piazza, the Winter Garden, a crystalline pavilion, acts as the conduit between the East River Science Park and Bellevue Hospital. The garden connects the two primary biotech facilities and functions as a performance or art gallery space.

ALEXANDRIA CENTER

IONA
COLLEGE
A Calling
to Teach
690
IONA
COLLEGE

Iona University Residence Hall

NEW ROCHELLE, NY
97,000 SF

At one time predominantly a commuter college, Iona's current on-campus population comprises 43 percent of all students with the demand of on-campus housing increasing each year. The university is committed to a goal of housing 60 percent of undergraduates on campus. The new residence hall houses an estimated 250 to 350 full-time students, while the street-level commercial space provides property tax income to the city and contributes to the revitalization of North Avenue.

The core of Iona's mission is to serve students, which is manifested in their desire to provide a "living and learning" environment. This beautiful and technologically advanced residence hall was designed to attract more students desiring a living and learning Iona experience and to strengthen and maintain Iona's close ties with the surrounding community.

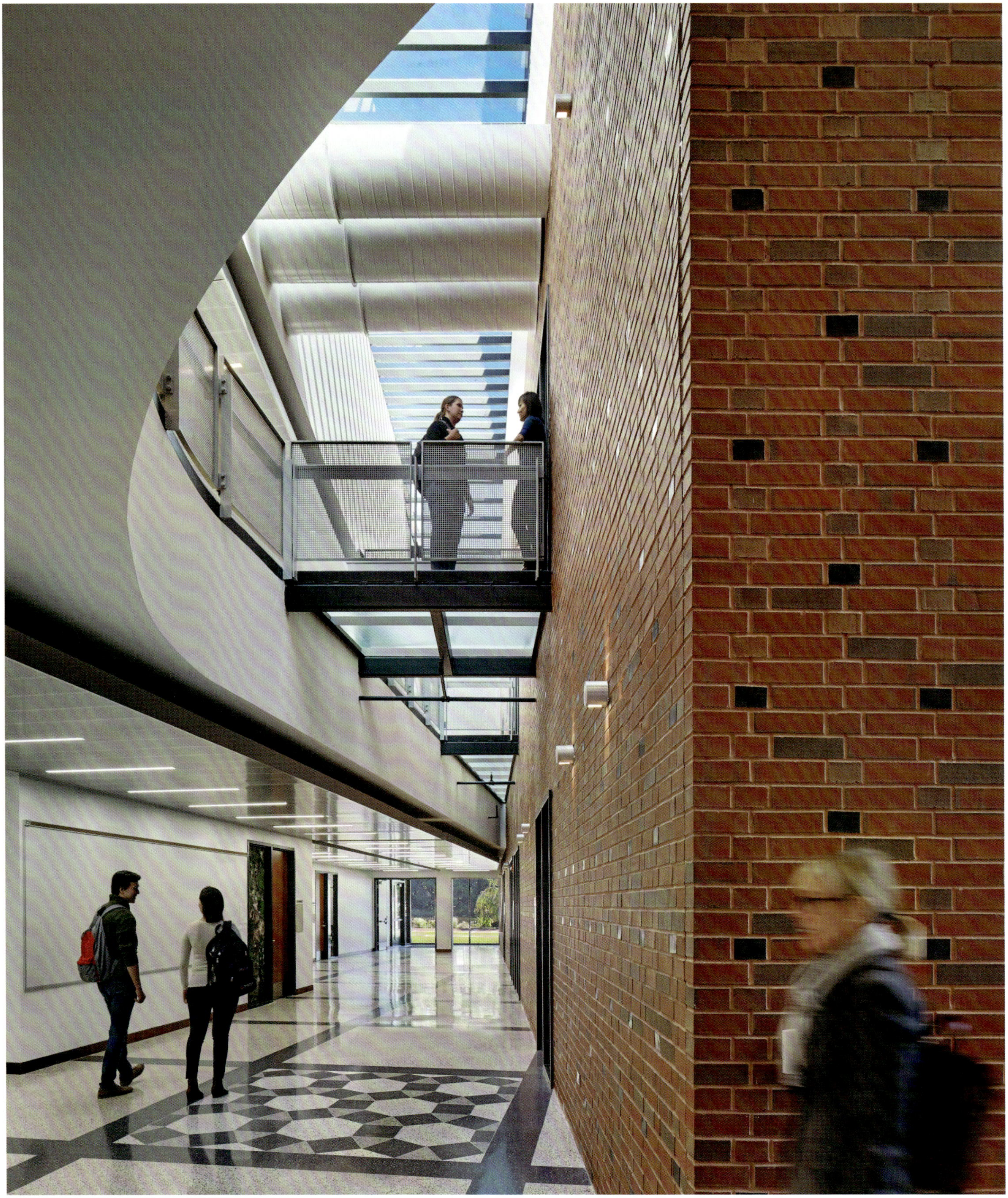

The Lawrenceville School Kirby Math and Science Center

LAWRENCEVILLE, NJ
30,000 SF

The F. M. Kirby Math and Science Center frames one of the three major greens on the famous Olmstead-designed prep school campus. The entrance incorporates "science on display" within an atrium that ties the Flagpole Green through to the football stadium. The student and faculty lounges, academic departments, and shared teaching spaces are arranged along a wide, bright, cross-axial corridor that connects to the existing computer science facility.

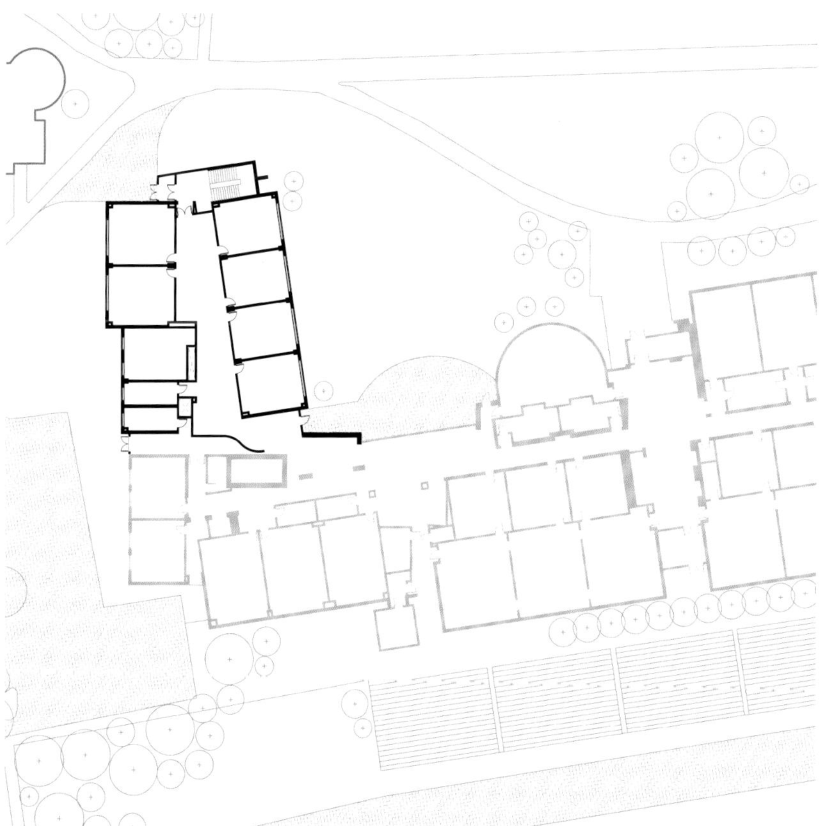

THE F. M. KIRBY MATH AND SCIENCE CENTER

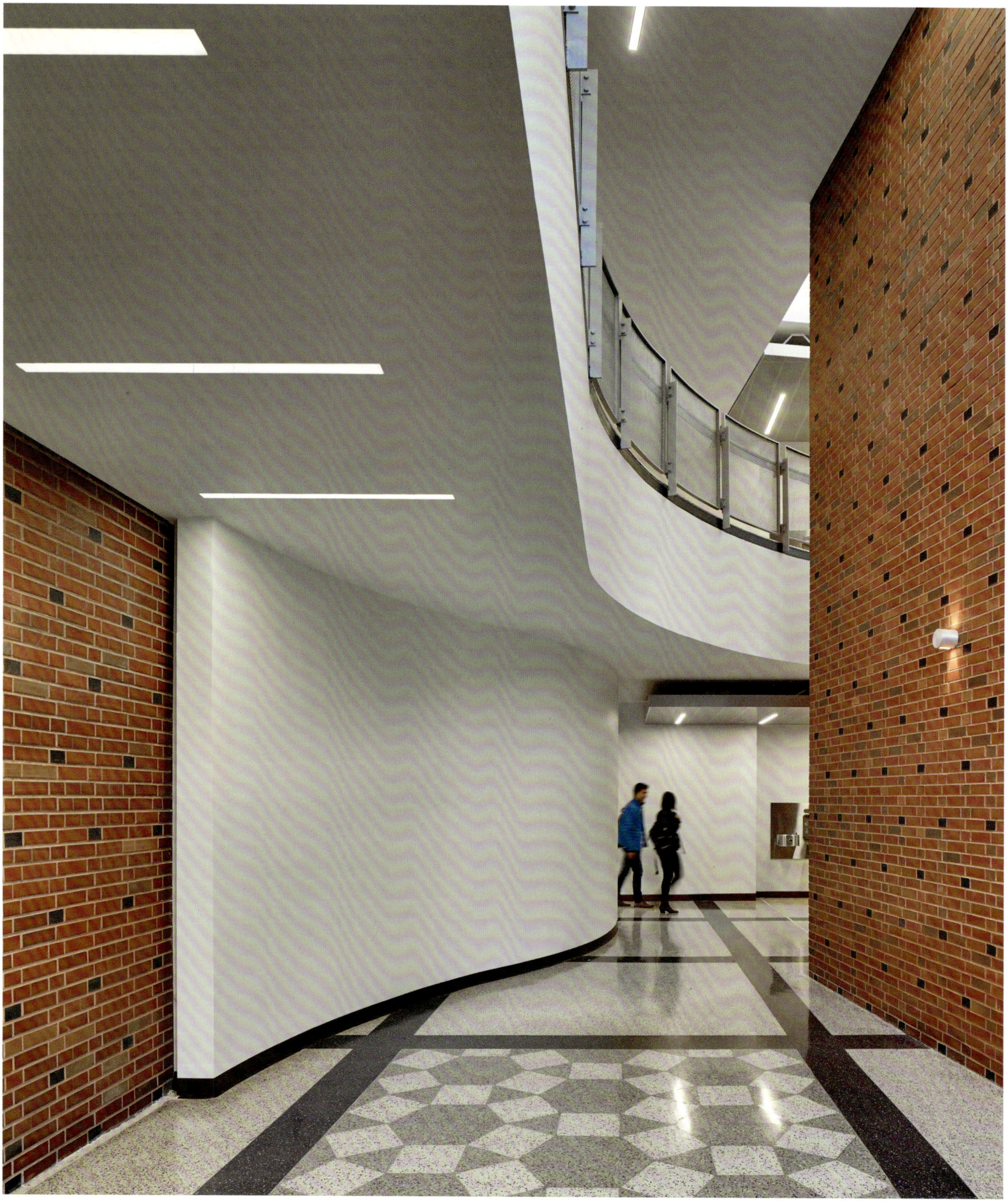

Fourteen years later, the school wished to add a wing to the Science Center that would replace the aging Corby Math Building. The two-story, 20,000-square-foot addition fulfilled the school's STEM objectives by adding new classrooms and creating a learning commons that unifies the interdisciplinary curriculum-based programs. The building materials used for the addition are a continuation of the patterned brick, cast stone, and zinc used in the original Kirby Science Center.

FINE WINE &
GOOD SPIRITS
PREMIUM COLLECTION
202A

Steeple View

NEWTOWN, PA
48,000 SF

Studio Hillier was the design architect for Steeple View, a mixed-use development in historic downtown Newtown, PA; at 48,000 square-feet, it was the largest infill project in the Borough in more than a decade and won the Award for Design Excellence, Large Project category, given by the Bucks County chapter of the AIA.

FINE WINE & GOOD SPIRITS

On the ground floor are two retail spaces and an elegant condominium lobby which leads to ten luxury condominiums on the second and third floors above. The condos range from 2,200 to 3,600 square feet and feature radiant floor heating, fireplaces, interior courtyards, and balconies. Expansive windows bring in natural light and contribute to an open and airy atmosphere.

The building's massing and use of brick were strategically chosen to both provide continuity with the historic streetscape and to tie into the updated, modern aesthetic introduced in town in recent years.

Institute for Advanced Study Faculty Housing

PRINCETON, NJ
24,000 SF

The Institute for Advanced Study commissioned a new community of sixteen faculty residences on a site that looks out over Princeton Battlefield Park. The new residences continue the Institute's historic commitment to modern architecture and provide an environment that responds to a modern lifestyle with their "Great Room" designs and open kitchens.

During phase one, eight faculty townhouses of approximately 3,000 square feet each were built at a total cost of $6.7 million. Each building has a full basement, patio, two aboveground living floors, and a ground-level two-car garage. The ground floor is composed of a living/dining room in an open-floor concept with a walk-out raised deck. The second floor has three bedrooms and two full bathrooms. Each townhouse has an elevator. Phase two, which is in progress, includes eight new townhouses to be constructed as a group of six plus two duplexes.

River Road Residence

NEW HOPE, PA
4,665 SF

Studio Hillier was commissioned to create a single-family home overlooking the Delaware River that would make the most of its surroundings while satisfying the owner's needs for their family and art collection. The new house was required to be completely above the 500-year flood level, and zoning disallowed any new construction on the ground level beyond the thirty-foot-by-30-foot footprint of the existing cottage, since removed.

As a result, the entire residence, supported by three fourteen-foot-high Vierendeel trusses, is lifted above the flood level and cantilevered over a concrete pedestal occupying the footprint of the original cottage. This poured concrete base contains a garage for three cars and a two-story high-entrance foyer with a view out to the river. In the event of a flood, vents open to allow water to pass through these spaces.

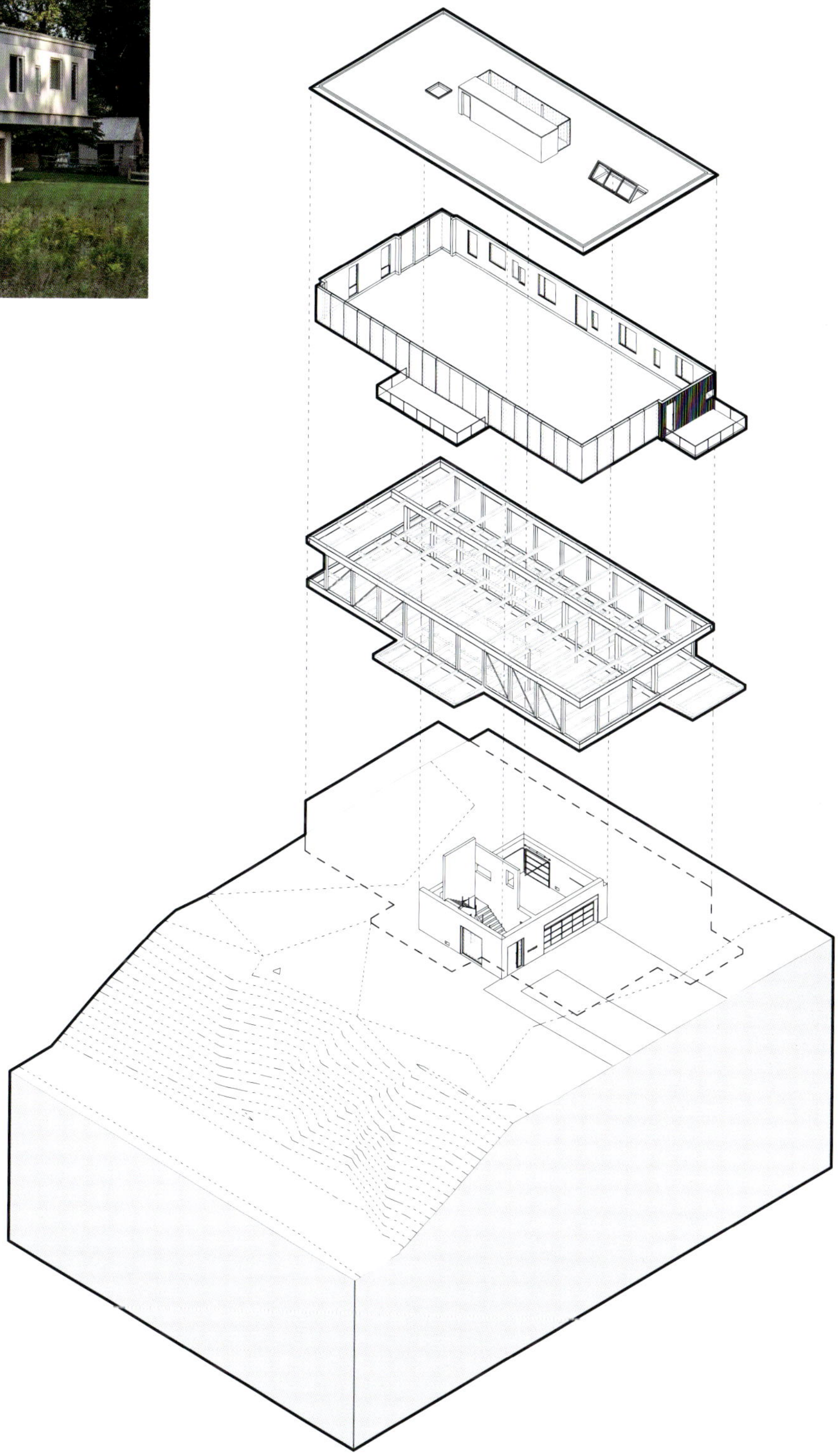

Conceived as a floating box alongside the Delaware River, the house experiences radical fluctuations in its environment in tandem with the river's ever-changing microclimate. Unique combinations of air temperature, water temperature, humidity, wind speed, and daylight create a fluid dialogue between the home and its surroundings. Spring mornings, for example, tend to be clear, with bright, warm daylight, while fall mornings are usually foggy with cooler-toned light. However, daily and hourly changes of the river allow occupants to experience a myriad of its conditions.

Nantucket Residence

NANTUCKET, MA
5,250 SF

One of the easternmost homes in all of Nantucket exhibits a minimalist approach to modern Danish architecture in a truly transformative redesign. An oceanfront property with a private path directly to the beach allows the client to awaken with the morning sunrise over the North Atlantic.

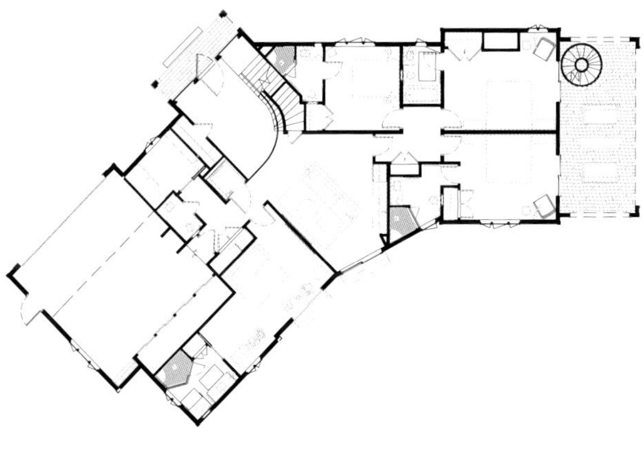

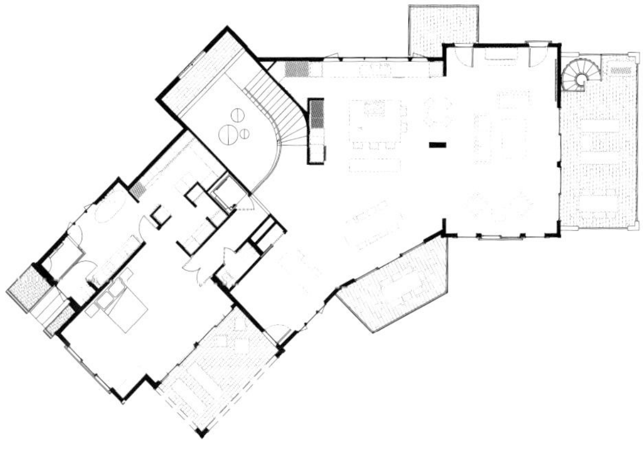

In harmony with the shore of Nantucket, expansive glass openings with minimalistic detailing bridge the connection between the indoor and outdoor space. Partition walls were removed to create an upper-level open floorplan that allows natural light to flow throughout the space. The second floor was designed to be a gathering space around the centralized open-plan kitchen, while taking advantage of the breathtaking 360-degree views. The cantilevered second floor balconies also open to scenic northeastern views.

The vacation home features private quarters located on the first floor with a private bath for each suite. The centralized kitchenette and wine bar services the private bedrooms on the first floor with a full-service gym in the corner. When the sun sets, guests can keep warm around a covered natural gas firepit while overlooking views to the sea.

Project Credits

AUTRETEMPS

Design Team:
J. Robert Hillier, Barbara Hillier

Consultant Team:
Executive Architect: Andrew Sheldon
General Contractor: Lucien Peebles
Structural Engineer: Harrison-Hamnett, PC

LVMH HEADQUARTERS

Client:
LVMH, Louis Vuitton Moët Hennessy Group

Design Team:
Christian de Portzamparc, Bruno Durbecq, J. Robert Hillier, Barbara Hillier, Guy Geier, James Greenberg, Peter Marino, John Mulliken, Philip Toussaint, Barbara Zieve

Consultant Team:
General Contractor:
Tishman Construction Corporation
Structural Engineer:
Weiskopf and Pickworth
MEP Engineer: Lilker Associates
Lighting: Fisher Marantz Stone
Geotechnical *Engineer:* Langan
Curtain Wall Engineer: R. A. Heintges
Zoning Consultant: Michael Parley
Owner/Developer: Franklin E. Dickinson

GLAXOSMITHKLINE GLOBAL HEADQUARTERS

Client:
GlaxoSmithKline

Design Team:
J. Robert Hillier, Hank Abernathy, Mark Chen, Mike Darvill, Rob Ellis, Len Groom, Sedge Hahm, Susan Hodges, Rob Leslie, Stephen Pargiter, Craig Perry, John Price, Carl Quinn, Amit Rabheru, Dave Seager, Karin Smit, Martin West, Mark Zihler

Consultant Team:
Associate Architect:
RHWL Architects and Swanke Hayden Connell Architects
Project Manager: Gardiner & Theobald Management Services
Construction Manager: Mace Group
Structural Engineer:
WSP Consulting Engineers
Fire Protection System:
Jeremy Gardner Associates
IT: Coleman Bennett International
Foodservice Consultants:
Rentokil Initial UK Limited
Data Cabling Consultant: Coleman Bennett International Plc - Site
Archaeological Survey: Museum of London Archaeological Survey
EDMS: C3 Systems Limited

HOWARD UNIVERSITY STOKES LIBRARY

Client:
Howard University

Design Team:
J. Robert Hillier, Bill DuBois, Peter Hoggan, Charles J. Maira, Joe Rizzo, Debbie Rockey, Joseph G. Tattoni

Consultant Team:
Associate Architect:
Amos, Bailey and Lee Ltd.
Civil & Structural: Jackson & Tull
MEP/F: Loring Engineering
AV/IT: Daou Systems
Lighting: The Lighting Practice
Cost Estimating: Daedulus
Acoustics: Acentech

General Contractor: Beta Construction
Construction Manager:
Blue Skye Construction, LLC
Landscape Architect: Susan Child

SOLEBURY SCHOOL ABBE SCIENCE CENTER

Client:
The Solebury School

Design Team:
Barbara Hillier, J. Robert Hillier, José A. Atienza, Charlie Maira, Despina Raggousis, Bradley Walters, Kevin Westerbeck

Consultant Team:
General Contractor/Construction Manager: E. Allen Reeves, Inc.
Structural/MEP:
Greenman-Pedersen, Inc.
Lighting: Grenald Waldron Associates
Landscape:
Van Cleef Engineering Associates

CORNELL UNIVERSITY LABORATORY OF ORNITHOLOGY

Client:
Cornell University

Design Team:
J. Robert Hillier, Alan Chimacoff, Nicholas Garrison, Peter Hoggan, Ken Kraus, Charlie Maira, Debbie Rockey, Sal Tomasello

Consultant Team:
Civil Engineer: Costich Engineering
Structural Engineer:
Robert Silman Associates, P.C.
MEP Engineer/Tele Data:
VanZelm Engineers LLC
Landscape Architect: Child Associates
Environmental Consultant: International Engineering
& Development Corporation
Acoustics/Audio Visual:
Acentech Incorporated

THE WAXWOOD

Client:
Robinhood Plaza

Design Team:
J. Robert Hillier, Barbara Hillier, Meredith Bostwick-Lorenzo Eiroa, Kate Goggin, David Moos

Consultant Team:
Civil Engineer:
R.L. Showalter & Associates
Structural Engineer:
Harrison - Hamnet, P.C.
MEP Engineer:
Pressman & Associates, Inc.
Landscape Architect:
D. Thomas Stearns
Fire Sprinkler Engineer: Aquatech, Inc.
Fire Alarm Engineer:
Loss Control Associates, Inc.

HOUSE AT LEESIDE FARM

Design Team:
J. Robert Hillier, Jennifer Akerman, José Atienza, Matt Baab, Gabe Czako, Meredith Bostwick-Lorenzo Eiroa, Royce Epstein, Kimberly MacKenzie, Bradley Walters, Erika Weidner

Consultant Team:
General Contractor:
Gordon H. Baver, Inc.
Civil Engineer:
Showalter & Associates
Structural Engineer:
Harrison-Hamnett, P.C.
MEP Engineer:
Syska Hennessy Associates
Landscape Architect: Janet Garwood

Soils and Geotechnical Engineer:
DelVal Soil
& Environmental Consultants
Specifications:
Thomas Fulmer and Jeffrey Wilson

PEDDIE SCHOOL ANNENBERG SCIENCE CENTER

Client:
Peddie School

Design Team:
J. Robert Hillier, John Bosio,
James Burton, Royce Epstein,
Bob DeGenova, Steve McDaniel,
Amy Rees, Jim Theodore

Consultant Team:
Structural Engineer: Reuther+Bowen
Mechanical Engineer:
Vanderweil Engineers

DUKE NUS SINGAPORE

Client:
Duke University/
National University of Singapore

Design Team:
J. Robert Hillier, Steven Gifford,
Peter Schubert
Consultant Team:
CPG Consultants Pte. Ltd

PRINCETON PUBLIC LIBRARY

Client:
Town of Princeton, Leslie Burger

Design Team:
J. Robert Hillier, John Bosio,
Nicholas Garrison, Peggy Keherer,
Joe Rizzo, Donna Terzano,
Luis Vildostegui

Consultant Team:
Civil /Structural Engineers:
French & Parrello Associates, P.A.
MEP Engineers: Paul H. Yeoman's Inc.
Construction Manager:
Turner Construction
Cost Estimates:
International Consultants, Inc.
Acoustical: Accentech, Inc. *Audiovisual:*
Nassoura Technology Associates
Security: Aggleton & Associates

SYNYGY WORLD HEADQUARTERS

Client:
The Buccini/Pollin Group, Inc.

Design Team:
J. Robert Hillier, Sonia Bijelic,
Mimi Campbell, Royce Epstein,
Rob Flaymik, Susan Kessler,
Jeffrey Mooney

Consultant Team:
Associate Architect: Blackney Hayes
General Contractor:
A&E Construction Co.
Structural Engineer: CVM Engineers
MEP Engineer: Devine Brothers w/
Jon Edward Fox & Assoc.,
Syska Hennessy Group
Electrical: Robert Ford Electric
Lighting: Syska Hennessy Group
Historical: Martin Jay Rosenblum, RA
& Associates, Kise Straw & Kolodner
Demolition: Central Salvage Co., Inc.

NEW JERSEY MEDICAL SCHOOL CANCER CENTER

Client:
The University of Medicine
and Dentistry of New Jersey,
David C. Shultz, AIA, Vice President
of Administration

Design Team:
J. Robert Hillier, Jan Bishop,
Greg Weiland, Colin Mosher,
Jack Mus, Russel Swanson,
Phillip Toussaint

Consultant Team:
Civil: Greenman-Pederson Inc.
Structural Engineer: Reuther+Bowen
MEP: Bard, Rao + Athans
Construction Manager:
Turner Construction Company
Acoustics: Cerami and Associates
Laboratory Planner: Bob Degenova
Cost Estimating: VJ Associates
Interior Design: Jessica Vuocolo

DUKE UNIVERSITY FRENCH SCIENCE CENTER

Client:
Duke University
Jim Churchman, Vice President

Design Team:
J. Robert Hillier, Laura Carlson,
Ron Eiswerth, Steve Gifford,
Tom Goodhart, Frank Theyssen,
Jim Theodore

Consultant Team:
Design Architect: Moore Ruble Yudell
General Contractor:
Skanska USA Building, Inc
Civil Engineer:
The John R. McAdams Company
Structural: LeMessurier Consultants
MEP: Bard, Rao + Athanas

Landscape Architect:
OLIN Partnership
Laboratory Planner:
AHSC McLellan Copenhagen
Code Consultant: Harold R. Cutler
Greenhouse Consultant:
Graham Hubenthal Architects

CENTRAL PARK NORTH

Client:
Athena Group

Design Team:
J. Robert Hillier, Barbara Hillier, Steven Gifford, Roger Goodhill, James Jenkins, Peter Schubert

Consultant Team:
Associate Architect:
SLCE Architects LLP
Construction: Bolvis Lend Lease

QUARRY STREET TWO-PLEX

Design Team:
J. Robert Hillier, Jennifer Akerma, David Moos, Daniel A. Ward

Consultant Team:
Site/Civil Engineer:
Van Note-Harvey Associates

BECTON DICKINSON CAMPUS CENTER

Client:
Becton, Dickinson and Company

Design Team:
Barbara Hillier, Jennifer Akerman, José Atienza, Martin Bloomenthal, Philip M. Donovan, Janet Garwood, Ernie Hunt, Margaret "Peggy" Kehrer, Michael Levin, Despina Raggousis, George Swallow; Bradley Walters, Evan Yassky

Consultant Team:
Civil Engineer:
Owen, Little + Associates
Structural Engineer:
Leslie E. Robertson Associates
MEO/F Engineer: AKF Engineers, LLP
Audio/Visual, Tele/Data & Security:
AKF Technologies
Lighting: Brandston Partnership Inc.
Vegetated Roof Specialist:
Roofscapes, Inc.

Waterproofing:
Simpson Gumpertz & Heger
Food Facilities: Post & Grossbard
Construction Manager: Gilbane

GOUCHER COLLEGE ATHENAEUM

Client:
Goucher College

Design Team:
J. Robert Hillier, Nicholas Garrison, Kenneth Kraus, Karl Pettit, Joe Rizzo, Bradley Walters

Consultant Team:
Civil Engineer:
Draft McCune Walker, Inc.
Structural Engineer:
A. W. Lookup Corp.
MEP: RMF Engineering
Lighting: George Sexton Associates
Construction Manager:
Whiting-Turner Contracting, Co.

IRVING CONVENTION CENTER

Client:
City of Irving, Texas

Design Team:
Barbara Hillier, Andy Buchsbaum, Kenneth Coupe, Gregory Dilly, Ernie Hunt, Michael Jaeger, Eric Jaffe, Sara Segal, Sal Tomaselli, Bradley Walters, Brian Wong, Winston Yeo, Gregory Zilli

Consultant Team:
Civil Engineer:
Jacobs Carter Burgess Engineers
Structural Engineers:
Datum Gojer Engineers
MEP Engineer:
RG Vanderweil Engineers
Lighting: Illumination Arts
Landscape Architect: Lisa Roth
Geotechnical Engineer: Terracon
Construction Manager:
Austin Commercial
A/V, IT, Security: Emmaco Prentiss
Food Service: Theodore Barber and Co.
Fountain Design: Wet Design
Curtainwall/Rainscreen:
Zahner Company
Parking Structure:
Walter P. Moore & Associates

Graphic Signage: Barbara Hillier
Vertical Circulation: Lerch Bates
Irrigation: Texas Irrigation Design
Facility and Food & Beverage Operations: SMG/Savor Worldwide
MWBE: The Burrell Group
Copper Cladding: Zahner
Steel Fabricators: W&W Steel and North Texas Steel
Steel Detailer: International Design Services, Inc.
Steel Erector: Bosworth Steel Erectors

URBAN TRIFECTA

Client:
Hillier Properties

Design Team:
J. Robert Hillier, Barbara Hillier, Jennifer Ackerman, Jack Mus

Consultant Team:
Civil Engineer: Van Note Harvey
Structural Engineer: Harrison -Hamnett P.C.
Mechanical Engineers: M&E Engineers

PENN MEDICINE PRINCETON MEDICAL CENTER

Client:
Penn Medicine

Design Team:
HOK
J. Robert Hillier, Jan Bishop, John Bosio, Colin Mosher, Jack Mus, Russell L. Swanson, Philip Touissant, Jessica Vuocolo, Greg Weiland

Consultant Team:
Civil Engineer: French & Parrello Associates
Structural Engineer: O'Donnell & Naccarato, Inc.
MEP Engineer: Syska Hennessy Group
Construction Manager: Turner Construction
CCHP Engineer: Concord Engineering

SOLEBURY TWO-PLEX

Design Team:
J. Robert Hillier, Jack Mus, Sumit Sahdev

Consultant Team:
Civil Engineer: Langan
Structural Engineer: Harrison-Hamnett, P.C.

COPPERWOOD

Client:
Cooperwood Associates - Shamco Management

Design Team:
J. Robert Hillier, Barbara Hillier, Kenneth Coupe, Felix Heidgen, Myles McCaulay, Jack Mus, Terayama Nagy, Benjamin Pollak, Shingo T., Sumit Sahdev

Consultant Team:
General Contractor: Costanza Builders
Civil Engineer: Van Note Harvey
Structural Consultant: Harrison - Hamnett, P.C.
MEP Engineer: Costanza Builders, Inc.
Electrical Consultant: Energy Squared, LLC
Landscape Consultant: Stephen A. Lederach, CLA
Fire Sprinkler Consultant: A.S. Barlin Associates, Inc.
Acoustics Consultant: Shen Milsom & Wilke SM & W

EAST RIVER SCIENCE PARK

Client:
Alexandria Real Estate Equities, Inc.

Design Team:
J. Robert Hillier, Barbara Hillier, James Butterfield, Steven Gifford, Peter Schubert

Consultants:
General Contractor: Turner Construction
Developer: Nancy J. Kelley + Associates
Civil Engineer: Vollmer Associates
Structural Engineer: Severud Associates
Mechanical Engineer: Jaros Baum & Bolles
Landscape Architect: Hargreaves Associates
Geotechnical: Musser Rutledge
Parking/Traffic: Sam Schwartz LLC

IONA UNIVERSITY RESIDENCE HALL

Client:
Iona University

Design Team:
J. Robert Hillier, Barbara Hillier, Dan Bolohan, Tsvetelina Churalska, Julian Edgren, James Estrada, James Giresi, Felix Heidgen, Myles McCaulay, Jack Mus, Benjamin Pollak, David Schragger, Sara Shonk, William M. Zaynor

Consultant Team:
General Contractor:
EWHOWELL Construction Group
Civil: Langan
Structural: Reuther + Brown
MEP: ST Engineering Services LLP

THE LAWRENCEVILLE SCHOOL KIRBY MATH AND SCIENCE CENTER

Client:
The Lawrenceville School

Design Team:
J. Robert Hillier, Barbara Hillier, Dan Bolohan, Andrew Buchsbaum, Tsvetelina Churalska, Kenneth Coupe, James Giresi, Felix Heidgen, Jack Mus, Sumit Sahdev, David Schragger, Sara Shonk, Benjamin Pollak, William M. Zaynor

Consultant Team:
Civil Engineer Consultant:
The Reynolds Group, Inc.
Structural Consultant: Reuther+Bowen
MEP Engineer: AKF
Audio/Visual Consultant: AKF
Landscape Consultant:
LRSLA Studio, Inc.

STEEPLE VIEW

Client:
Steeple View Limited Partnership

Design Team:
J. Robert Hillier, Felix Heidgen, David Schragger

Consultant Team:
Civil Engineer:
Gilmore & Associates, Inc.
Structural Engineer: Reuther+Bowen
Construction Manager:
C. Raymond Davis & Sons

INSTITUTE FOR ADVANCED STUDY FACULTY HOUSING

Client:
Institute for Advanced Study

Design Team:
J. Robert Hillier, Barbara Hillier, Dylan Belfield, Dan Bolohan, Tsvetelina Churalska, James Giresi, Felix Heidgen, Myles McCauley, David Schragger, Charles Sharpless, Sara Shonk, William M. Zanyor

Consultant Team:
General Contractor:
Sweetwater Construction Corp.
Civil Engineer:
Van Note-Harvery Associates, P.C.
Structural Engineer:
Harrison-Hamnett, P.C
MEP Engineer:
Keller & Gilligo Consulting Engineers
Landscape Architect:
Stearns Associates, LLC
Hydraulic Engineer: Langan

RIVER ROAD RESIDENCE

Design Team:
J. Robert Hillier, Barbara Hillier, Dylan Belfield, Dan Bolohan, Tsvetlina Churalska, Julian Edgren, James Giresi, Vivian Scherer, David Schragger, Sara Shonk, Christina Tiam, Benjamin Pollak, William M. Zaynor

Consultant Team:
Structural Engineer:
Harrison - Hamnett, P.C
Civil Engineer/Land Survey: Langan
Geotechnical Engineer:
Melick-Tully and Associates

NANTUCKET RESIDENCE

Design Team:
J. Robert Hillier, Barbara Hillier, Dustin Bailey, Dan Bolohan, Tsvetlina Churalska, Julian Edgren, Felix Heidgen, Alyson Rock, Hiei Rose, David Schragger, William M. Zaynor

Consultant Team:
General Contractor:
Main Street Construction
Structural Engineer: Lee H. Dunn, Inc.
MEP Engineer: T.E. McGrath Plumbing & Heating, Inc.
Cabinet Consultant:
Nayaug & Co., LLC

Every reasonable effort has been made to credit the team members of projects included in this monograph. Any errors and omissions that may have occurred are inadvertent.

Acknowledgments

To all of our clients and friends who have supported us all of these years—we are grateful for all the opportunities and thank you for encouraging us along the way. Without your support and trust, Hillier would not be the name that it is today. We are also indebted to our past and current employees. The collective talents of former principals, associate principals, senior associates, associates, architects, interns, and staff over the years at J. Robert Hillier Architects, The Hillier Group, Hillier Architecture, and Studio Hillier have contributed to our shared success and growth. We are deeply grateful for everyone's commitment to design and quality in bringing our projects to life.

We would like to specially thank our internal monograph team, Julian Edgren, Caryn Farnum, Alexander Kim, Julia Stanat, and Kaitlyn Zook, for their efforts in compiling and preparing images from the archives, writing text, guiding the design, and telling our story. We would also like to thank interns, Nikita Goswami and Justin Mortman, as well as Zachery Mangan for assisting in the reproduction of all sketches and drawings.

We want to acknowledge and thank all our collaborators. We specially thank Stan Allen for his thoughtful and insightful words in the foreword; Gordon Goff and his team at ORO Editions for guiding and supporting us through this endeavor; and Pablo Mandel, from CircularStudio, for visually and graphically supporting our story. Finally, thank you to all the photographers who have captured our projects with breathtaking images for this monograph.

Bob and Barbara Hillier

About Studio Hillier

Studio Hillier LLC is an interdisciplinary design firm in Princeton, NJ, cofounded in 2011 by partners Barbara A. Hillier, AIA, and J. Robert Hillier, LHD, FAIA, PP. Together for more than forty years, they have formed the backbone of a vibrant, growing, full-service architectural studio that has the depth of experience and design talent to take on a challenge of any scope.

They work collaboratively with experts who bring excellence and robust knowledge of the latest building technologies including prefabrication, environmental systems, and the preservation of historic structures. Their success is reflected in the number of repeat clients who recognize their rigorous standards of performance in meeting occupancy dates, managing the budget, and delivering high-quality design and professional services. With over 350 design awards, their reputation for excellence is evidence of their commitment to their clients, to place, to sustainability, and to the built environment.

About the Hilliers

J. ROBERT HILLIER is an American architect known for his speaking and teaching about architecture as well as for his prolific range of completed works in thirty-four states and twenty-two countries. He built his firm, Hillier Architecture (previously The Hillier Group), into one of the most successful architecture firms in the country before merging with an international firm to become one of the world's largest. In 2010, he and his wife established Studio Hillier, a new firm focusing on community need, neighborhood enhancement, and special opportunities for architectural interventions.

Bob, as he is known to friends and colleagues, was born in Toronto, Ontario, but basically grew up in Princeton, NJ, one of two sons of high-achieving parents. His father was James Hillier, a leading scientist for RCA who is credited with designing and building the first successful scanning electron microscope; his mother, Florence Hillier, owned three flower shops around town. He graduated from Princeton Day School, the Lawrenceville School, and Princeton University, where he received both a Bachelor of Arts and a Master of Architecture degree.

From an early age, Bob's entrepreneurial instinct was apparent; at age thirteen he was running a lucrative business selling tropical fish to Princeton students through his mother's flower shops to pay for half the cost of attending Lawrenceville, an agreement he made with his father. During his undergraduate years at Princeton, he was a campus politician and a class officer and designed decorations for many of the school's proms. His advisor, recognizing the evident design talent, suggested architecture as a course of study.

After receiving his architecture degree, he worked briefly for a local architecture firm before opening his own office on Nassau Street in 1966. His first job was replacing a bathroom vanity for a wealthy Princeton man, but that soon turned into a commission to renovate the client's corporate office building in Chicago. From there, the firm expanded rapidly, delivering numerous award-winning projects for clients throughout New Jersey and the Northeast.

By 1980, the firm had hired its one hundredth employee; by 1987, The Hillier Group was the country's seventh largest architectural firm with a staff of 235. A full-service regional office was opened in Philadelphia in 1988 under the leadership of Design and Managing Principal Barbara Hillier, Bob's wife. By the 2000s, Hillier Architecture was an industry leader recognized as one of the best-managed firms by *Architectural Record* and had offices in New York, Princeton, Philadelphia, Washington, DC, Shanghai, and Dubai. Its portfolio includes award-winning headquarters for many of the largest companies in Europe and the United States, works for major universities, state-of-the-art research laboratories for industry leaders as well as mixed-use hotel, residential and office complexes in the United States and Asia.

Rather than adopting a particular style or even basic doctrines of design within his firm, Hillier promotes a working environment where each designer is empowered to find their own way in pursuit of quality and excellence. To deliver the kind of design that each market sector looks for, Hillier Architecture was divided into thirteen practice groups, such as laboratories, historic preservation, higher education, and interior design. Hillier culture is rooted in a philosophy of celebrating the extraordinary differences among people and places while responding to them with sensitivity and respect.

In addition to running a successful business, since 1992, Bob has been on the core faculty of Princeton University's School of Architecture, where he teaches two graduate seminars about the business of architectural practice. In a school that emphasizes theory, the course is widely known as "Bob's reality check." He has served as chair of the Selection Committee for the dean of Princeton's School of Architecture as well as on the AIA National Fellowship Jury, having been elevated to Fellowship in 1976.

At the New Jersey Institute of Technology, Bob's influence and impact are especially visible. The original architecture school's renovation was designed by Hillier in 1972, and the school's own building was designed by Hillier in 1999. He has also been on NJIT's Board of Overseers since 1993. In 2009 he was awarded the NJIT President's Medal for Lifetime Achievement and in 2017 received an honorary doctor of humane letters. In May 2019, the architecture school was renamed the J. Robert and Barbara A. Hillier College of Architecture and Design following a transformative gift from the Hilliers.

In 2007, J. Robert Hillier was awarded the AIA New Jersey Michael Graves Lifetime Achievement Medal, given "in recognition of a significant body of work of lasting influence on the theory and practice of architecture."

BARBARA A. HILLIER was born in Philadelphia, PA to Shirley and Coleman Feinberg. Early on in her education, Barbara displayed an aptitude for creative artistry, which her high school guidance counselor suggested could make her a successful hair stylist. But Barbara was unpersuaded by her counselor's prediction for her future. Instead, she attained a Psychology degree from Temple University followed by a BFA in Interior/Graphic Design from Arcadia University.

In 1976, armed with two degrees but no experience in architectural design, Barbara began her career as an interior designer at J. Robert Hillier, Architect, a small, Princeton-based design firm. She opened the firm's regional office in Philadelphia in 1988 and led a studio grounded in strong architecture, planning, and interior design work. She worked for many years without a professional degree before becoming a licensed architect in Pennsylvania in 1993 having completed the required 13 years of specific architectural work experience.

After helping build the firm to national and international prominence and becoming a mother, Barbara returned to school in 2011, and met her lifetime dream of completing her professional education with an M. Arch at Princeton University.

Over the past four decades, Barbara's architectural projects have been celebrated for creatively synthesizing innovation and performance. Her human-centric approach empowers clients and stakeholders while driving her design toward unexpected solutions. She challenges her design teams to ask difficult questions and challenge the status quo.

For example, Barbara's Irving Convention Center is a vertically stacked landscape of meeting rooms that defies typological conventions. At the Becton Dickinson Campus Center, a conventional building connecting two existing ones was reimagined as an insertion under a treasured central lawn to preserve it while still fulfilling a connective function between the marketing and research and development departments...over lunch. The Solebury School Abbe Science Center is a sustainable, technologically advanced facility that adroitly engages the historic context and materials of the region.

Barbara begins with people. Then, she thoughtfully layers context, history, and the particulars of place into her solution. Her sensitive approach to design creates spaces that are responsive, provocative, and inspirational. Her projects have been published widely and influenced other architects who have followed in her footsteps. Her work has been recognized with numerous awards from AIA chapters including the coveted Pennsylvania AIA Silver Medal and The Chicago Athenaeum Award.

Given her own unconventional educational path to architecture, Barbara believes in an inclusive design education that engages students, professionals, and the public. She has lectured extensively and served on numerous academic and professional design juries, including as Chair of the 2001 AIA National Honor Awards Jury for Interior Design. In Philadelphia in 2002, Barbara created and led a series of ten public lectures in which notable architects such as Enrique Norten and Wes Jones participated. She has also served on the Boards of Trustees of Philadelphia University of the Arts and the Philadelphia Foundation for Architecture.

Eager to share her expertise and knowledge, Barbara has relentlessly mentored generations of architects and designers. In 1979, she created "Hillier Career Day." Beginning with six high school students, it grew to include over a hundred students by 2000. This initiative raised local awareness of the profession and launched the architectural careers for many students including 17 participants who later became Hillier employees. Barbara also led the Hillier Intern Program, which was recognized at the 2000 AIA National Convention and is responsible for leading many architects to successful careers in top firms.

In 2019, New Jersey Institute of Technology's architecture school was renamed the J. Robert and Barbara A. Hillier College of Architecture and Design, celebrating the Hilliers' commitment to providing more equitable access to design education. NJIT has been ranked #1 nationally by Forbes Magazine for Student Upward Mobility.

Photography Credits

AUTRETEMPS
Julian Edgren

LVMH TOWER
Paul Warchol Photography

GLAXOSMITHKLINE GLOBAL HEADQUARTERS
© Edmund Sumner

HOWARD UNIVERSITY STOKES LIBRARY
© Peter Mauss/Esto

SOLEBURY SCHOOL ABBE SCIENCE CENTER
© Albert Vecerka/Esto

CORNELL UNIVERSITY LABORATORY OF ORNITHOLOGY
© Brad Feinknopf/OTTO

THE WAXWOOD
Julian Edgren

HOUSE AT LEESIDE FARM
© Albert Vecerka/Esto

PEDDIE SCHOOL ANNENBERG SCIENCE CENTER
© Albert Vecerka/Esto

DUKE NUS SINGAPORE
Infinitude

PRINCETON PUBLIC LIBRARY
Julian Edgren

SYNYGY WORLD HEADQUARTERS
© Jeffry Totaro / Jeffrey E. Tyron

NEW JERSEY MEDICAL SCHOOL CANCER CENTER
© Peter Brown Architectural Photography

DUKE UNIVERSITY FRENCH SCIENCE CENTER
© Robert Benson Photography

CENTRAL PARK NORTH
Jeffrey E. Tyron / Julian Edgren

QUARRY STREET TWO-PLEX
Thomas Kieren

BECTON DICKINSON CAMPUS CENTER
© Brad Feinknopf/OTTO

GOUCHER COLLEGE ATHENAEUM
Jeffrey E. Tyron

IRVING CONVENTION CENTER
Tex Jernigan/ARKO

PENN MEDICINE PRINCETON MEDICAL CENTER
Richard Titus Photographics

SOLEBURY TWO-PLEX
Jeffrey E. Tyron

URBAN TRIFECTA
Halkin/Mason Photography

COPPERWOOD
Tom Grimes Photography

EAST RIVER SCIENCE PARK
Julian Edgren

IONA UNIVERSITY RESIDENCE HALL
Halkin/Mason Photography

THE LAWRENCEVILLE SCHOOL KIRBY MATH AND SCIENCE CENTER
Halkin/Mason Photography

STEEPLE VIEW
Don Pearse Photographers, Inc.

INSTITUTE FOR ADVANCED STUDY FACULTY HOUSING
Halkin/Mason Photography

RIVER ROAD RESIDENCE
Julian Edgren

NANTUCKET RESIDENCE
Julian Edgren

Every reasonable effort has been made to credit the ownership of copyright for images included in this monograph. Any errors that may have occurred are inadvertent.

Contributors

Stan Allen
Stan Allen is an architect and George Dutton '27 Professor of Architecture at Princeton University and former Dean of the School of Architecture. His practice, Stan Allen Architect, has realized buildings and urban projects in the United States, South America, and Asia. Responding to the contemporary city in creative ways, Allen has developed an extensive catalogue of innovative design strategies, in particular looking at field theory, landscape architecture, and ecology as models to revitalize design practice. Parallel to this large-scale work he has recently completed a number of private houses and artist's studios on rural sites in the Hudson River Valley. His architectural work is published in *Points + Lines: Diagrams and Projects for the City* and his essays in *Practice: Architecture, Technique and Representation.* The edited volume *Landform Building: Architecture's New Terrain* was published by Lars Müller in 2011, and his most recent book is *Situated Objects*, published by Park Books in 2020.

Pablo Mandel
Pablo is an Argentine-Canadian graphic designer. For more than two decades he has built a career designing books on architecture; working with renown architects, universities, musicians, and artists in the United States, Canada, Australia, Japan, Singapore, China, Italy, Germany, England, Spain, Chile, and Argentina. Born in Argentina in 1970, Pablo graduated from Buenos Aires University in 1995 with a degree in Graphic Design, emigrating to Canada shortly after. His book designs have been published internationally and have been the recipient of numerous awards, including the Canadian Society of Landscape Architects' National Merit Award 2011 for *Grounded*, and for *Moving Landscapes* (2016); and the Bookbuilders West's Certificate of Excellence (Image-driven trade books, 2009, 2010, 2011). In parallel to his graphic design activity, Pablo has been active for more than 20 years as a musician, member of the League of Crafty Guitarists and the Guitar Circles. Last but not least: Pablo is an artist, a husband, and a father.